DIARIES OF COURT LADIES

OF OLD JAPAN

COURT LADY'S FULL DRESS IN THE HEIAN PERIOD
(For explanation see List of Illustrations)

DIARIES OF COURT LADIES
OF OLD JAPAN

TRANSLATED BY
ANNIE SHEPLEY OMORI
AND
KOCHI DOI
Professor in the Tohoku Imperial University, Sendai

WITH AN INTRODUCTION BY
AMY LOWELL

And with Illustrations

KENKYUSHA CO.
Fujimi-cho, Kojimachi-ku, Tokyo
1935

PRINTED IN JAPAN BY KENKYUSHA CO., TOKYO

CONTENTS

v

ILLUSTRATIONS

From *Kokushi Daijiten*, by kind permission of the editor,
Mr. H. Yoshikawa. The figure was drawn for the purpose of
showing the details of dress and therefore gives no indication
of the grace and elegance of the costume as worn. It shows
the red *karaginu*, or over-garment; the dark-green robe
trimmed with folds, called the *uchigi*; the *saishi*, or head-orna-
ment, in this case of gold but sometimes of silver; the unlined
under-garment of thin silk; the red *hakama*, or divided skirt;
and the train of white silk painted or stained in colours.

The above two pictures are taken from an ancient picture
scroll *Murasaki-Shikibu-Niki-Emaki*. The reproductions are
made from the negatives kindly lent to the translators by Mr.
R. Fukui, Professor of the Oriental Art in the Imperial
University of Sendai.

INTRODUCTION

By Amy Lowell

THE Japanese have a convenient method of calling their historical periods by the names of the places which were the seats of government while they lasted. The first of these epochs of real importance is the Nara Period, which began A.D. 710 and endured until 794 ; all before that may be classed as archaic.[1] Previous to the Nara Period, the Japanese had been a semi-nomadic race. As each suc cessive Mikado came to the throne, he built himself a new palace, and founded a new capital ; there had been more than sixty capitals before the Nara Period. Such shifting was not conducive to the development of literature and the arts, and it was not until a permanent government was established at Nara that these began to flourish. This is scarcely the place to trace the history of Japanese litera-ture, but fully to understand these charming " Diaries of Court Ladies of Old Japan," it is necessary to know a little of the world they lived in, to be able to feel their atmosphere and recognize their allusions.

We know a good deal about Japan to-day, but the Japan with which we are familiar only slightly resembles that of the Diaries. Centuries of feudalism, of " Dark Ages," have come between. We must go behind all this and

---

1 Miss Lowell evidently did not know the Asuka Period which cannot be classed as archaic, while Hōriuji remains to be seen, built by the Prince-Regent Shōtoku in the Asuka Period. What the age of the Primitifs was to Europe the Asuka Period was to Japan.

begin again. We have all heard of the "Forty-seven Ronins" and the Nō Drama, of Shōguns, Daimios, and Samurais, and many of us live in daily communion with Japanese prints. It gives us pause to reflect that the earliest of these things is almost as many centuries ahead of the Ladies as it is behind us. "Shōgun" means simply "General," and of course there were always generals, but the power of the Shōguns, and the military feudalism of which the Daimios and their attendant Samurais were a part, did not really begin until the middle of the twelfth century and did not reach its full development until the middle of the fourteenth; the Nō Drama started with the ancient religious pantomimic dance, the Kagura, but not until words were added in the fourteenth century did it become the No; and block colour printing was first practised in 1695, while such famous print artists as Utamaro, Hokusai, and Hiroshigé are all products of the eighteenth or early nineteenth centuries. To find the Ladies behind the dark military ages, we must go back a long way, even to the century before their own, and so gain a sort of perspective for them and their time.

Chinese literature and civilization were introduced into Japan somewhere between 270 and 310 A.D., and Buddhism followed in 552. Of course, all such dates must be taken with a certain degree of latitude; Oriental historians are anything but precise in these matters. Chinese influence and Buddhism are the two enormous facts to be reckoned with in understanding Japan, and considering what an effect they have had, it is not a little singular that Japan has always been able to preserve her native character. To be sure, Shintoism was never displaced by Buddhism,

Introduction

but the latter made a tremendous appeal to the Japanese temperament, as the Diaries show. In fact, it was not until the Meiji Period (1867-1912) that Shintoism was again made the state religion. With the introduction of Chinese civilization came the art of writing, when is not accurately known, but printing from movable blocks followed from Korea in the eighth century. As was inevitable under the circumstances, Chinese came to be considered the language of learning. Japanese scholars wrote in Chinese. All the " serious " books—history, theology, science, law—were written in Chinese as a matter of course. But, in 712, a volume called " Records of Ancient Matters " was compiled in the native tongue. It is the earliest book in Japanese now extant.

If the scholars wrote in a borrowed language, the poets knew better. They wrote in their own, and the poetry of the Nara Period has been preserved for us in an anthology, the " Manyoshu " or " Collection of Ten Thousand Leaves." This was followed at the beginning of the tenth century by the " Kokinshu " (" Ancient and Modern Poems "), to which, however, the editor, Tsurayuki, felt obliged to write a Chinese preface. The Ladies of the Diaries were extremely familiar with these volumes, their own writings are full of allusions to poems contained in them ; Sei Shōnagon, writing early in the eleventh century, describes a young lady's education as consisting of writing, music, and the twenty volumes of the " Kokinshu." So it came about that while learned gentlemen still continued to write in Chinese, poetry, fiction, diaries, and desultory essays called " Zuihitsu " (Following the Pen) were written in Japanese.

Introduction

Now the position of women at this time was very different from what it afterwards became in the feudal period. The Chinese called Japan the " Queen Country," because of the ascendancy which women enjoyed there. They were educated, they were allowed a share of inheritance, and they had their own houses. It is an extraordinary and important fact that much of the best literature of Japan has been written by women. Three of these most remarkable women are the authors of the Diaries ; a fourth to be named with them, Sei-Shōnagon, to whom I have just referred, was a contemporary.

In 794, the capital was moved from Nara to Kiōto, which was given the name of " Heian-jo " or " City of Peace," and with the removal, a new period, the Heian, began. It lasted until 1186, and our Ladies lived in the very middle of it.

By this time Japan was thoroughly civilized ; she was, indeed, a little over-civilized, a little too fined down and delicate. At least this is true of all that life which centred round the court at Kiōto. To historians the Heian Period represents the rise and fall of the Fujiwara family. This powerful family had served the Mikados from time out of mind as heads of the Shinto priests, and after the middle of the seventh century, they became ministers or prime ministers. An immense clan, they gradually absorbed all the civil offices in the Kingdom, while the military offices were filled by the Taira and Minamoto families. It was the rise of these last as the Fujiwara declined which eventually led to the rule of the Shōguns and the long centuries of feudalism and civil war. But in the middle of the Heian Period the Fujiwara were very much everywhere. Most of those Court ladies who were the authors of remarkable books were the daughters of governors of provinces, and that meant Fujiwaras to a greater or lesser degree. At that time polygamy flourished in Japan, and the family had grown to a prodigious size. Since a civil office meant a post for a Fujiwara, many of them were happily provided for, but they were so numerous that they outnumbered the legitimate positions and others had to be created to fill the demand. The Court was full of persons of both sexes holding sinecures, with a great deal of time on their hands and nothing to do in it but write poetry, which they did exceedingly well, and attend the various functions prescribed by etiquette. Ceremonials were many and magnificent, and poetry writing became, not only a game, but a natural adjunct to every possible event. The Japanese as a nation are dowered with a rare and exquisite taste, and in the Heian Period taste was cultivated to an amazing degree. Murasaki Shikibu records the astounding pitch to which it had reached in a passage in her diary. Speaking of the Mikado's ladies at a court festivity, she says of the dress of one of them : " One had a little fault in the colour combination at the wrist opening. When she went before the Royal presence to fetch something, the nobles and high officials noticed it. Afterwards Lady Saisho regretted it deeply. It was not so bad ; only one colour was a little too pale."

That passage needs no comment ; it is completely illuminating. It is a paraphrase of the whole era.

Kioto was a little city, long one way by some seventeen thousand odd feet, or about three and a third miles, wide the other by fifteen thousand, or approximately another three miles, and it is doubtful if the space within the city wall was ever entirely covered by houses. The Palace was built in the so-called Azumaya style, a form of architecture which was also followed in noblemen's houses. The roof, or rather roofs, for there were many buildings, was covered with bark, and, inside, the divisions into rooms were made by different sorts of moving screens. At the period of the Diaries, the reigning Mikado, Ichijo, had two wives : Sadako, the first queen, was the daughter of a previous prime minister, Michitaka, a Fujiwara, of course ; the other, Akiko, daughter of Michinaga, the prime minister of the Diaries and a younger brother of Michitaka, was second queen or Chūgū. These queens each occupied a separate house in the Palace. Kokiden was the name of Queen Sadako's house ; Fujitsubu the name of Queen Akiko's. The rivalry between these ladies was naturally great, and extended even to their *entourage*. Each strove to surround herself with ladies who were not only beautiful, but learned. The bright star of Queen Sadako's court was Sei-Shōnagon, the author of a remarkable book, the " Makura no Sōshi " or " Pillow Sketches," while Murasaki Shikibu held the same exalted position in Queen Akiko's.

We are to imagine a court founded upon the Chinese model, but not nearly so elaborate. A brilliant assemblage of persons all playing about a restricted but very bright centre. From it, the high officials went out to be governors of distant provinces, and the lesser ones followed them to minor posts, but in spite of the distinction of such positions, distance and the inconvenience of travelling made the going a sort of laurelled banishment. These gentlemen left Kiōto with regret and returned with satisfaction. But the going, and the years of residence away, was one of the commonplaces of social life. Fujiwara though one might be, one often had to wait and scheme for an office, and the Diaries contain more than one reference to such waiting and the bitter disappointment when the office was not up to expectation.

These functionaries travelled with a large train of soldiers and servants, but, with the best will in the world, these last could not make the journeys other than tedious and uncomfortable. Still there were alleviations, because of the very taste of which I have spoken. The scenery was often beautiful, and whether the traveller were the Governor himself or his daughter, he noticed and delighted in it. The "Sarashina Diary" is full of this appreciation of nature. We are told of "a very beautiful beach with long-drawn white waves," of a torrent whose water was "white as if thickened with rice flour." We need only think of the prints with which we are familiar to be convinced of the accuracy of this picture : "The waves of the outer sea were very high, and we could see them through the pine-trees which grew scattered over the sandy point which stretched between us and the sea. They seemed to strike across the ends of the pine branches and shone like jewels." The diarist goes on to remark that " it was an interesting sight," which we can very well believe, since certainly she makes us long to see it.

These journeys were mostly made on horseback, but there were other methods of progression, which, however, were probably not always feasible for long distances.

Introduction

The nobles used various kinds of carriages drawn by one
bullock, and there were also palanquins carried by bearers.

It was not only the officials who made journeys, all the
world made them to temples and shrines for the good of
their souls. There are religious yearnings in all the Diaries,
and many Mikados and gentlemen entered the priesthood,
Michinaga among them. Sutra recitation and incantation
were ceaselessly performed at Court. We can gain some
idea of the almost fanatical hold which Buddhism had over
the educated mind by the fact that the Fujiwara family
built such great temples as Gokurakuji, Hosohoji, Hokoin,
Jomyoji, Muryoju-in, etc. It is recorded that Mikado
Shirakawa, at a date somewhat subsequent to the Diaries,
made pilgrimages four times to Kumano, and during his
visit there "worshipped 5470 painted Buddhas, 127
carved Buddhas sixteen feet high, 3,150 Buddhas life-
sized, 2,930 carved Buddhas shorter than three feet, 21
pagodas, 446,630 miniature pagodas." A busy man
truly, but the record does not mention what became of the
affairs of state meanwhile. That this worship was by no
means lip-devotion merely, any reader of the "Sarashina
Diary" can see; that it was mixed with much superstition and a profound belief in dreams is also abundantly
evident. But let us, for a moment, recollect the time.
It will place the marvel of this old, careful civilization
before us as nothing else can.

To be sure, Greece and Rome had been, but they had
passed away, or at least their greatness had, gone and
apparently left no trace. While these Japanese ladies
were writing, Europe was in the full blackness of her
darkest ages. Germany was founding the "Holy Roman

Introduction

Empire of the German Nation," characteristically founding it with the mailed fist; Moorish civilization was at its
height in Spain; Robert Capet was king of poor famine-
scourged France; Ethelred the Unready was ruling in
England and doing his best to keep off the Danes by pay-
ment and massacre. Later, while the " Sarashina Diary "
was being written, King Canute was sitting in his armchair
and giving orders to the sea. Curious, curious world!
So far apart from the one of the Diaries. And to think
that even five hundred years later Columbus was sending
letters into the interior of Cuba, addressed to the Emperor
of Japan!

These Diaries show us a world extraordinarily like our
own, if very unlike in more than one important particular.
The noblemen and women of Mikado Ichijō's Court were
poets and writers of genius, their taste as a whole has never
been surpassed by any people at any time, but their scienti-
fic knowledge was elementary in the extreme. Diseases
and conflagrations were frequent. In a space of fifty-one
years, the Royal Palace burnt down eleven times. During
the same period, there were four great pestilences, a
terrible drought, and an earthquake. Robbers infested many
parts of the country, and were a constant fear to travellers
and pilgrims. Childbirth was very dangerous. The
picture of the birth of a child to Queen Akiko, with
which Murasaki Shikibu's Diary begins, shows us all its
bitter horror. From page to page we share the writer's
suspense, and with our greater knowledge, it is with a
sense of wonder that we watch the queen's return to health.

But, after all, diseases and conflagrations are seldom
more than episodes in a normal life lived under sane condi-

tions, and it is just because these Diaries reflect the real life of these three ladies that they are important. The world they portray is in most ways quite as advanced as our own, and in some, much more so. Rice was the staple of food, and although Buddhistic sentiment seldom permitted people to eat the flesh of animals, they had an abundance of fish, which was eaten boiled, baked, raw, and pickled, and a quantity of fruits and nuts. There was no sugar, but cakes were made of fruit and nuts, and there was always rice-wine or saké. Gentlefolk usually dressed in silk. They wore many layers of coloured garments, and delighted in the harmony produced by the colour combinations of silk over silk, or of a bright lining subdued by the tone of an outer robe. The ladies all painted their faces, and the whole toilet was a matter of sufficient moment to raise it into a fine art. Many of these lovely dresses are described by Murasaki Shikibu, for instance : "The beautiful shape of their hair, tied with bands, was like that of the beauties in Chinese pictures. Lady Saemon held the King's sword. She wore a blue-green patternless karaginu and shaded train with floating bands and belt of ' floating thread ' brocade dyed in dull red. Her outer robe was trimmed with five folds and was chrysanthemum coloured. The glossy silk was of crimson ; her figure and movement, when we caught a glimpse of it, was flower-like and dignified. Lady Ben-no-Naishi held the box of the King's seals. Her uchigi was grape-coloured. She is a very small and smile-giving person and seemed shy and I was sorry for her. . . .Her hair bands were blue-green. Her appearance suggested one of the ancient dream-maidens descended from heaven." A little later she tells us

Introduction

that " the beaten stuffs were like the mingling of dark and light maple leaves in Autumn " ; and, describing in some detail the festivity at which these ladies appeared, she makes the comment that " only the right body-guard wore clothes of shrimp pink." To one in love with colour, these passages leave a very nostalgia for the bright and sophisticated Court where such things could be.

And everywhere, everywhere, there is poetry. A gentleman hands a lady a poem on the end of his fan and she is expected to reply in kind within the instant. Poems form an important part in the ritual of betrothal. A daughter of good family never allowed herself to be seen by men (a custom which appears to have admitted many exceptions). A man would write a poetical love-letter to the lady of his choice which she must answer amiably, even should she have no mind to him. If, however, she were happily inclined, he would visit her secretly at night and leave before daybreak. He would then write again, following which she would give a banquet and introduce him to her family. After this, he could visit her openly, although she would still remain for some time in her father's house. This custom of love-letter writing and visiting is shown in Izumi Shikibu's Diary. Obviously the poems were short, and here, in order to understand those in the text, it may be well to consider for a moment in what Japanese poetry consists.

Japanese is a syllabic language like our own, but, unlike our own, it is not accented. Also, every syllable ends with a vowel, the consequence being that there are only five rhymes in the whole language. Since the employment of so restricted a rhyme scheme would be unbearably

monotonous, the Japanese hit upon the happy idea of
counting syllables. Our metrical verse also counts syllables, but we combine them into different kinds of accented feet. Without accent, this was not possible, so the
Japanese poet limits their number and uses them in a
pattern of alternating lines. His prosody is based upon
the numbers five and seven, a five-syllable line alternating
with one of seven syllables, with, in some forms, two
seven-syllable lines together at the end of a period, in the
manner of our couplet. The favourite form, the " tanka,"
is in thirty-one syllables and runs five, seven, five, seven,
seven. There is a longer form, the " naga-uta," but it
has never been held in as high favour. The poems in the
Diaries are all tankas in the original. It can be seen that
much cannot be said in so confined a medium, but much
can be suggested, and it is just in this art of suggestion
that the Japanese excel. The " hokku " is an even
briefer form. In it, the concluding hemistich of the tanka
is left off, and it is just in his hemistich that the meaning
of the poem is brought out, so that the hokku is a mere
essence, a whiff of an idea to be created in full by the hearer.
But the hokku was not invented until the fifteenth century;
before that, the tanka, in spite of occasional attempts to
vary it by adding more lines, changing their order, using
the pattern in combination as a series of stanzas, etc.,
reigned practically supreme, and it is still the chief classic
form for all Japanese poetry.

Having briefly washed in the background of the Diaries,
we must notice, for a moment, the three remarkable ladies
who are the foreground.

Murasaki Shikibu was the daughter of Fujiwara Tame-

Introduction

toki, a scion of a junior branch of the famous family. She was born in 978. Murasaki was not her real name, which was apparently To Shikibu (Shikibu is a title) derived from that of her father. There are two legends about the reason for her receiving the name Murasaki. One is that she was given it in playful allusion to her own heroine in the " Genji Monogatari," who was called Murasaki. The other legend is more charming. It seems that her mother was one of the nurses of Mikado Jchijo, who was so fond of her that he gave her daughter this name in reference to a well-known poem :
" When the purple grass (Murasaki) is in full colour,
    One can scarcely perceive the other plants in the field."
From the Murasaki grass, the word has come to mean a colour which includes all the shades of purple, violet, and lavender. In 996, or thereabouts, she accompanied her father to the Province of Echizen, of which he had become governor. A year later, she returned to Kioto, and, within a twelvemonth, married another Fujiwara, Nobutaka. The marriage seems to have been most happy, to judge from the constant expressions of grief in her Diary for her husband's death, which occurred in 1001, a year in which Japan suffered from a great pestilence. A daughter was born to them in 1000. From her husband's death, until 1005, she seems to have lived in the country, but in this year she joined the Court as one of Queen Akiko's ladies ; before that, however (and again I must insist that these early dates are far from determined), she had made herself famous, not only for her own time, but for all time, by writing the first realistic novel of Japan. This book is the " Genji Monogatari " or " Narrative of

Introduction

Genji."

Hitherto, Japanese authors had confined themselves to stories of no great length, and which relied for their interest on a fairy or wonder element. The "Genji Monogatari" struck out an entirely new direction. It depicted real life in Kioto as a contemporary gentleman might have lived it. It founded its interest on the fact that people like to read about themselves, but this, which seems to us a commonplace, was a glaring innovation when Murasaki Shikibu attempted it ; it was, in fact, the flash from a mind of genius. The book follows the life of Prince Genji from his birth to his death at the age of fifty-one, and the concluding books of the series pursue the career of one of his sons. It is an enormous work, comprising no less than fifty-four books and running to over four thousand pages —the genealogical tree of the personages alone is eighty pages long—but no reader of the Diary will need to be convinced that the " Genji " is not merely sprightly and captivating, but powerful as well. The lady was shrewd, and if she were also kindly and very attractive, nevertheless she saw with an uncompromising eye. Her critical faculty never sleeps, and takes in the nimutest detail of anything she sees, noting unerringly every little rightness and wrongness connected with it. She watches the approach of the Mikado, and touches the matter so that we get its exact shade : " When the Royal palanquin drew near, the bearers, though they were rather honourable persons, bent their heads in absolute humility as they ascended the steps. Even in the highest society there are grades of courtesy, but these men were too humble."

No one with such a gift can fail to be lonely, and Mura-

Introduction

saki Shikibu seems very lonely, but it is not the passionate rebellion of Izumi Shikibu, nor the abiding melancholy of the author of the " Sarashina Diary " ; rather is it the disillusion of one who has seen much of the world, and knows how little companionship she may expect ever to find : " It is useless to talk with those who do not understand one and troublesome to talk with those who criticize from a feeling of superiority. Especially one-sided persons are troublesome. Few are accomplished in many arts and most cling narrowly to their own opinion."

I have already shown Murasaki Shikibu's beautiful taste in dress, but indeed it is in everything. When she says " The garden [on a moonlight night] was admirable," we know that it must have been of an extraordinary perfection.

The Diary proves her dramatic sense, as the " Genji " would also do could it find so sympathetic a translator. No wonder, then, that it leapt into instant fame. There is a pretty legend of her writing the book at the Temple of Ishiyama at the southern end of Lake Biwa. The tale gains verisimilitude in the eyes of visitors by the fact that they are shown the chamber in the temple in which she wrote and the ink-slab she used, but, alas ! it is not true. We do not know where she wrote, nor even exactly when. The " Genji " is supposed to have been begun in 1002, and most commentators believe it to have been finished in 1004. That she should have been called to Court in the following year, seems extremely natural. Queen Akiko must have counted herself most fortunate in having among her ladies so famous a person.

The Diary tells the rest, the Diary which was begun in

1007. We know no more of Murasaki Shikibu except that no shade of scandal ever tinged her name.

One of the strangest and most interesting things about the Diaries is that their authors were such very different kinds of people. Izumi Shikibu is as unlike Murasaki Shikibu as could well happen. As different as the most celebrated poet of her time is likely to be from the most celebrated novelist, for Izumi Shikibu is the greatest woman poet which Japan has had. The author of seven volumes of poems, this Diary is the only prose writing of hers which is known. It is an intimate account of a love affair which seems to have been more than usually passionate and pathetic. Passionate, provocative, enchanting, it is evident that Izumi Shikibu could never have been the discriminating observer, the critic of manners, which Murasaki Shikibu became. Life was powerless to mellow so vivid a personality; but neither could it subdue it. She gives us no suggestion of resignation. She lived intensely, as her Diary shows; she always had done so, and doubtless she always did. We see her as untamable, a genius compelled to follow her inclinations. Difficult to deal with, maybe, like strong wine, but wonderfully stimulating.

Izumi Shikibu was born in 974. She was the eldest daughter of Ōe Masamune, another Governor of Echizen. In 995, she married Tachibana Michisada, Governor of Izumi, hence her name. From this gentleman she was divorced, but just when we do not know, and he died shortly after, probably during the great pestilence which played such havoc throughout Japan and in which Murasaki Shikibu's husband had also died. Her daughter, who followed in her mother's footsteps as a poet, had been born in 997. But Izumi Shikibu was too fascinating and too petulant to nurse her disappointment in a chaste seclusion. She became the mistress of Prince Tametaka, who also died in 1002. It is very soon after this event that the Diary begins. Her new lover was Prince Atsumichi, and the Diary seems to have been written solely to appease her mind, and to record the poems which passed between them and which Izumi Shikibu evidently regarded as the very essence of their souls.

In the beginning, the affair was carried on with the utmost secrecy, but clandestine meetings could not satisfy the lovers, and at last the Prince persuaded her to take up her residence in the South Palace as one of his ladies. Considering the manners of the time, it is a little puzzling to see why there should have been such an outcry at this, but outcry there certainly was. The Princess took violent umbrage at the Prince's proceeding and left the Palace on a long visit to her relations. So violent grew the protestations in the little world of the Court that, in 1004, Izumi Shikibu left the Palace and separated herself entirely from the Prince. It was probably to emphasize the definiteness of the separation that, immediately after her departure, she married Fujiwara Yasumasa, Governor of Tango, and left with him for that Province in 1005. The facts bear out this supposition, but we do not know it from her own lips, as the Diary breaks off soon after she reaches the South Palace.

In 1008, she was summoned back to Kioto to serve the Queen in the same Court where Murasaki Shikibu had been since 1005. Whatever effect the scandal may have had

Introduction

four years earlier, her receiving the post of lady-in-waiting
proves it to have been worth forgetting in view of her fame,
and Queen Akiko must have rejoiced to add this celebrated
poet to her already remarkable bevy of ladies.   Of course
there was jealousy—who can doubt it ?   No reader of the
Diaries can imagine that Izumi Shikibu and Murasaki
Shikibu can have been sympathetic, and we must take with
a grain of salt the latter's caustic comment : " Lady Izumi
Shikibu corresponds charmingly, but her behavior is
improper indeed.   She writes with grace and ease and a
flashing wit.   There is a fragrance even in her smallest
words.   Her poems are attractive, but they are only improvisations which drop from her mouth spontaneously.
Every one of them has some interesting point, and she is
acquainted with ancient literature also, but she is not like
a true artist who is filled with the genuine spirit of poetry.
Yet I think even she cannot presume to pass judgment on
the poems of others."   Is it possible that Izumi Shikibu
had been so rash as to pass judgment on some of Murasaki
Shikibu's efforts ?

Of course it is beyond the power of any translation to
preserve the full effect of the original, but even in translation, Izumi Shikibu's poems are singularly beautiful and
appealing.   In her own country, they are considered never
to have been excelled in freshness and freedom of expression.   There is something infinitely sad in this, which she
is said to have written on her death-bed, as the end of a
passionate life :

> " Out of the dark,
> Into a dark path

Introduction

I now must enter :
Shine [on me] from afar
Moon of the mountain fringe."[1]

In Japanese poetry, Amita-Buddha is often compared to the moon which rises over the mountains and lights the traveller's path.

Very different again is the lady who wrote the " Sarashina Diary," and it is a very different kind of record. Murasaki Shikibu's Diary is concerned with a few years of her life, Izumi Shikibu's with one episode only of hers, but the " Sarashina Diary " covers a long period in the life of its author. The first part was written when she was twelve years old, the last entry was made when she was past fifty. It begins with a journey from Shimōsa to Kioto by the Tōkaidō in 1021, which is followed by a second journey some years later from Kioto to Sarashina, a place which has never been satisfactorily identified, although some critics have supposed it to have been in the Province of Shinano. The rest of the Diary consists of jottings at various times, accounts of books read, of places seen, of pilgrimages to temples, of records of dreams and portents, of communings with herself on life and death, of expressions of resignation and sorrow.

The book takes its name from the second of the journeys, " Sarashina Nikki," meaning simply " Sarashina Diary," for, strangely enough, we do not know the author's name. We do know, however, that she was the daughter of Fujiwara Takasué, and that she was born in 1009. In 1017, Takasué was appointed governor of a province, and went

[1] Translation by Arthur Waley in *Japanese Poetry*.

with his daughter to his new post. It is the return journey, made in 1021, with which the Diary opens.

Takasué's daughter shared with so many of her contemporaries the deep love of nature and the power to express this love in words. I have already quoted one or two of her entries on this journey. We follow the little company over mountains and across rivers, we camp with them by night, and tremble as they trembled lest robbers should attack them. We see what the little girl saw: " The mountain range called Nishitomi is like folding screens with good pictures," " people say that purple grass grows in the fields of Musashi, but it is only a waste of various kinds of reeds, which grow so high that we cannot see the bows of our horsemen who are forcing their way through the tall grass," and share her disappointment when she says : " We passed a place called ' Eight Bridges,' but it was only a name, no bridge and no pretty sight."

They reach Kioto and a rather dull life begins, enlivened only by the avid reading of romances, among them the " Genji Monogatari." Then her sister dies giving birth to a child, and the life becomes, not only dull, but sorrowful. After a time, the lady obtains a position at Court, but neither her bringing up nor her disposition had suited her for such a place. She mentions that " Mother was a person of extremely antiquated mind," and it is evident that she had been taught to look inward rather than outward. An abortive little love affair lightens her dreariness for a moment. Life had dealt hardly with the sensitive girl, from year to year she grows more wistful, but suddenly something happens, a mere hint of a gleam, but opening a possibility of brightness. Who he was, we do not know, but she met him on an evening when " there was no starlight, and a gentle shower fell in the darkness." They talked and exchanged poems, but she did not meet him again until the next year ; then, after an evening entertainment to which she had not gone, " when I looked out, opening the sliding door on the corridor, I saw the morning moon very faint and beautiful," and he was there. Again they exchanged poems and she believed that happiness had at last arrived. He was to come with his lute and sing to her. " I wanted to hear it," she writes, " and waited for the fit occasion, but there was none, ever." A year later she has lost hope, she writes a poem and adds, " So I composed that poem—and there is nothing more to tell." Nothing more, indeed, but what is told conveys all the misery of her deceived longing.

The last part of the Diary is concerned chiefly with accounts of pilgrimages and dreams. She married, who and when is not recorded, and bore children. Her husband dies, and with his death the spring of her life seems to have run down. Her last entry is very sad: " My people went to live elsewhere and I lived alone in my solitary home." So we leave her, " a beautiful, shy spirit whose life had known much sorrow."

I

THE SARASHINA DIARY

DIARIES OF
COURT LADIES OF OLD JAPAN

I

THE SARASHINA DIARY

A.D. 1009-1059

I WAS brought up in a distant province[1] which lies farther than the farthest end of the Eastern Road. I am ashamed to think that inhabitants of the Royal City will think me an uncultured girl.

Somehow I came to know that there are such things as romances in the world and wished to read them. When there was nothing to do by day or at night, one tale or another was told me by my elder sister or stepmother, and I heard several chapters about the shining Prince Genji.[2] My longing for such stories increased, but how could they recite them all from memory? I became very restless and got an image of Yakushi Buddha[3] made as large as myself. When I was alone I washed my hands and went secretly before the altar and prayed to him with all my life, bowing my head down to the floor.

[1] Her father Takasué was appointed Governor of Kazusa in 1017, and the authoress, who was then nine years old, was brought from Kyoto to the Province.

[2] Prince Genji: The hero of Genji-monogatari, a novel by Murasaki-Shikibu.

[3] Yakushi Buddha: "The Buddha of healing," or Sanscrit, Bhaisajya-guru-Vaiduryaprabhah.

3

" Please let me go to the Royal City. There I can find many tales. Let me read all of them."

When thirteen years old, I was taken to the Royal City. On the third of the Long-moon month,[1] I removed [from my house] to Imataté, the old house where I had played as a child being broken up. At sunset in the foggy twilight, just as I was getting into the palanquin, I thought of the Buddha before which I had gone secretly to pray—I was sorry and secretly shed tears to leave him behind.

Outside of my new house [a rude temporary, thatched one] there is no fence nor even shutters, but we have hung curtains and sudaré.[2] From that house, standing on a low bluff, a wide plain extends towards the South. On the East and West the sea creeps close, so it is an interesting place. When fogs are falling it is so charming that I rise early every morning to see them. Sorry to leave this place.

On the fifteenth, in heavy dark rain, we crossed the boundary of the Province and lodged at Ikada in the Province of Shimofusa. Our lodging is almost submerged. I am so afraid that I cannot sleep. I see only three lone trees standing on a little hill in the waste.

The next day was passed in drying our dripping clothes and waiting for the others to come up.[3]

[1] Original, Nagatsuki, September.

[2] Ancient ladies avoided men's eyes and always sat behind sudaré (finely split bamboo curtain) through which they could look out without being seen.

[3] High personages, Governors of Provinces or other nobles, travelled with a great retinue, consisting of armed horsemen, foot-soldiers, and attendants of all sorts both high and low, together with the luggage neces-

Of Old Japan

On the seventeenth, started early in the morning, and crossed a deep river. I heard that in this Province there lived in olden times a chieftain of Mano. He had thousand and ten thousand webs of cloth woven and dipped them [for bleaching] in the river which now flows over the place where his great house stood. Four of the large gate-posts remained standing in the river.

Hearing the people composing poems about this place, I in my mind :

> *Had I not seen erect in the river*
> *These solid timbers of the olden time*
> *How could I know, how could I feel*
> *The story of that house ?*

That evening we lodged at the beach of Kurodo. The white sand stretched far and wide. The pinewood was dark—the moon was bright, and the soft blowing of the wind made me lonely. People were pleased and composed poems. My poem :

> *For this night only*
> *The autumn moon at Kurodo beach shall shine for me,*
> *For this night only !—I cannot sleep.*

Early in the morning we left this place and came to the Futoi River[1] on the boundary between Shimofusa and Musashi. We lodged at the ferry of Matsusato[2] near Kagami's rapids,[3] and all night long our luggage was being carried over.

sary for prolonged existence in the wilderness. From Tokyo to Kioto nowadays the journey is about eight hours. It took about three months in the year 1017.

[1] Futoi River is called the River Edo at present.
[2] Matsusato, now called Matsudo.
[3] Kagami's rapids, now perhaps Karameki-no-se.

5

My nurse had lost her husband and gave birth to her child at the boundary of the Province, so we had to go up to the Royal City separately. I was longing for my nurse and wanted to go to see her, and was brought there by my elder brother in his arms. We, though in a temporary lodging, covered ourselves with warm cotton batting, but my nurse, as there was no man to take care of her, was lying in a wild place [and] covered only with coarse matting. She was in her red dress.

The moon came in, lighting up everything, and in the moonlight she looked transparent. I thought her very white and pure. She wept and caressed me, and I was loath to leave her. Even when I went with lingering heart, her image remained with me, and there was no interest in the changing scenes.

The next morning we crossed the river in a ferry-boat in our palanquins. The persons who had come with us thus far in their own conveyances went back from this place. We, who were going up to the Royal City, stayed here for a while to follow them with our eyes ; and as it was a parting for life all wept. Even my childish heart felt sorrow.

Now it is the Province of Musashi. There is no charm in this place. The sand of the beaches is not white, but like mud. People say that purple grass[1] grows in the fields of Musashi, but it is only a waste of various kinds of reeds, which grow so high that we cannot see the bows of our horsemen who are forcing their way through the tall grass. Going

[1] Common gromwell, *Lithospermum*.

through these reeds I saw a ruined temple called Takeshiba-dera. There were also the foundation-stones of a house with corridor.

"What place is it?" I asked; and they answered:

"Once upon a time there lived a reckless adventurer at Takeshiba.[1] He was offered to the King's palace [by the Governor] as a guard to keep the watch-fire. He was once sweeping the garden in front of a Princess's room and singing:

Ah, me! Ah, me! My weary doom to labour here in the Palace!
Seven good wine-jars have I—and three in my province.
There where they stand I have hung straight-stremmed gourds of
the finest—
  They turn to the West when the East wind blows,
  They turn to the East when the West wind blows,
  They turn to the North when the South wind blows,
  They turn to the South when the North wind blows.
And there I sit watching them turning and turning forever—
  Oh, my gourds! Oh, my wine-jars!

"He was singing thus alone, but just then a Princess, the King's favourite daughter, was sitting alone behind the misu.[2] She came forward, and, leaning against the doorpost, listened to the man singing. She was very interested to think how gourds were above the wine-jars and how they were turning and wanted to see them. She became very zealous for the gourds, and pushing up the blind

[1] Takeshiba: Now called Shibaura, place-name in Tokyo near Shinagawa. Another manuscript reads: "This was the manor house of Takeshiba."

[2] Misu: finer sort of sudaré used in court or in Shinto shrine. Cf. note 2, p. 4.

called the guard, saying, ' Man, come here ! ' The man heard it very respectfully, and with great reverence drew near the balustrade. ' Let me hear once more what you have been saying.' And he sang again about his wine-jars. ' I must go and see them, I have my own reason for saying so,' said the Princess.

" He felt great awe, but he made up his mind, and went down towards the Eastern Province. He feared that men would pursue them, and that night, placing the Princess on the Seta Bridge,[1] broke a part of it away, and bounding over with the Princess on his back arrived at his native place after seven days' and seven nights' journey.

" The King and Queen were greatly surprised when they found the Princess was lost, and began to search for her. Some one said that a King's guard from the Province of Musashi, carrying something of exquisite fragrance[2] on his back, had been seen fleeing towards the East. So they sought for that guard, and he was not to be found. They said, ' Doubtless this man went back home.' The Royal Government sent messengers to pursue them, but when they got to the Seta Bridge they found it broken, and they could not go farther. In the Third month, however, the messengers arrived at Musashi Province and sought for the man. The Princess gave audience to the messengers and said :

[1] Seta Bridge is across the river from Lake Biwa, some seven or eight miles from Kyoto.
[2] In those days noblemen's and ladies' dresses were perfumed.

8

" ' I, for some reason, yearned for this man's home and bade him carry me here ; so he has carried me. If this man were punished and killed, what should I do ? This is a very good place to live in. It must have been settled before I was born that I should leave my trace [i.e. descendants] in this Province— go back and tell the King so. ' So the messengers could not refuse her, and went back to tell the King about it.

" The King said : ' It is hopeless. Though I punish the man I cannot bring back the Princess; nor is it meet to bring them back to the Royal City. As long as that man of Takeshiba lives I cannot give Musashi Province to him, but I will entrust it to the Princess.'

" In this way it happened that a palace was built there in the same style as the Royal Palace and the Princess was placed there. When she died they made it into a temple called Takeshiba-dera.[1] The descendants of the Princess received the family name of Musashi. After that the guards of the watch-fire were women."[2]

We went through a waste of reeds of various kinds, forcing our way through the tall grass. There is the river Asuda along the border of Musashi and Sagami, *where at the ferry Arihara Narihira had composed his famous poem.*[3] In the book of his poetical works the river is called the river Sumida.

[1] Dera or tera = temple.

[2] The original text may also be understood as follows : " After that the guards of the watch-fire were allowed to live with their wives in the palace."

[3] In the *Isé-monogatari* (a book of Narihira's poetical works) the Sumida

We crossed it in a boat, and it is the Province of
Sagami. The mountain range called Nishitomi is
like folding screens with good pictures. On the left
hand we saw a very beautiful beach with long-drawn
curves of white waves. There was a place there
called Morokoshi-ga-Hara[1] [Chinese Field] where
sands are wonderfully white. Two or three days we
journeyed along that shore. A man said: " In
Summer pale and deep Japanese pinks bloom there
and make the field like brocade. As it is Autumn
now we cannot see them." But I saw some pinks
scattered about blooming pitiably. They said:
" It is funny that Japanese pinks are blooming in
the Chinese field."

There is a mountain called Ashigara [Hakoné]
which extends for ten and more miles and is covered
with thick woods even to its base. We could have
only an occasional glimpse of the sky. We lodged in

River is said to be on the boundary between Musashi and Shimofusa. So
the italicized words seem to be the authoress's mistake, or more probably
an insertion by a later smatterer of literary knowledge who inherited the
manuscript.

Narihira's poem is addressed to a sea-gull called *Miyakodori*, which literally means *bird of the capital*. Narihira had abandoned Kyoto and was wandering towards the East. Just then his heart had been yearning after the Royal
City and also after his wife, and that feeling must have been intensified by
the name of the bird. (Cf. The *Isé-monogatari*, Section 9.)

> *Miyakodori ! alas, that word*
> *Fills my heart again with longing,*
> *Even you I ask, O bird,*
> *Does she still live, my beloved?*

[1] According to " Sagami-Fudoki," or " The Natural Features of Sagami
Province," this district was in ancient times inhabited by Koreans. The
natives could not distinguish a Korean from a Chinese, hence the name of
Chinese Field. A temple near Ōiso still keeps the name of Kōraiji, or the
Korean temple.

a hut at the foot of the mountain. It was a dark moonless night. I felt myself swallowed up and lost in the darkness, when three singers came from somewhere. One was about fifty years old, the second twenty, and the third about fourteen or fifteen. We set them down in front of our lodging and a karakasa [large paper umbrella] was spread for them. My servant lighted a fire so that we saw them. They said that they were the descendants of a famous singer called Kobata. They had very long hair which hung over their foreheads ; their faces were white and clean, and they seemed rather like maids serving in noblemen's families. They had clear, sweet voices, and their beautiful singing seemed to reach the heavens. All were charmed, and taking great interest made them come nearer. Some one said, " The singers of the Western Provinces are inferior to them," and at this the singers closed their song with the words, " if we are compared with those of Naniwa " [Ōsaka][1] They were pretty and neatly dressed, with voices of rare beauty, and they were wandering away into this fearful mountain. Even tears came to those eyes which followed them as far as they could be seen ; and my childish heart was unwilling to leave this rude shelter frequented by these singers.

Next morning we crossed over the mountain.[2]

[1] This seems to be the last line of a kind of song called *Imayo*, perhaps improvised by the singers ; its meaning may be as follows : " You compare us with singers of the Western Provinces ; we are inferior to those in the Royal City ; we may justly be compared with those in Ōsaka."

[2] Hakoné Mountain has now become a resort of tourists and a place of summer residence.

Words cannot express my fear[1] in the midst of it. Clouds rolled beneath our feet. Halfway over there was an open space with a few trees. Here we saw a few leaves of aoi[2] [*Asarum caulescens*]. People praised it and thought strange that in this mountain, so far from the human world, was growing such a sacred plant. We met with three rivers in the mountain and crossed them with difficulty. That day we stopped at Sekiyama. Now we are in Suruga Province. We passed a place called Iwatsubo [rock-urn] by the barrier of Yokobashiri. There was an indescribably large square rock, through a hole in which very cold water came rushing out.

Mount Fuji is in this Province. In the Province where I was brought up [from which she begins this journey] I saw that mountain far towards the West. It towers up painted with deep blue, and covered with eternal snow. It seems that it wears a dress of deep violet and a white veil over its shoulders. From the little level place of the top smoke was going up. In the evening we even saw burning fires there.[3] The Fuji River comes tumbling down from that mountain. A man of the Province came up to us and told us a story.

" Once I went on an errand. It was a very hot day, and I was resting on the bank of the stream when I

---

[1] Fear of evil spirits which probably lived in the wild, and of robbers who certainly did.

[2] Aoi, or Futaba-aoi. At the great festival of the Kamo shrine in Kioto the processionists crowned their heads with the leaves of this plant, so it must have been well known.

[3] Mount Fuji was then an active volcano.

saw something yellow come floating down. It came
to the bank of the river and stuck there. I picked it
up and found it to be a scrap of yellow paper with
words elegantly written on it in cinnabar. Wondering much I read it. On the paper was a prophecy
of the Governors [of provinces] to be appointed next
year. As to this Province there were written the
names of two Governors. I wondered more and
more, and drying the paper, kept it. When the day
of the announcement came, this paper held no mistake, and the man who became the Governor of this
Province died after three months, and the other
succeeded him."

There are such things. I think that the gods as-
semble there on that mountain to settle the affairs of
each new year.

At Kiyomigasеki, where we saw the sea on the left,
there were many houses for the keepers of the barriers. Some of the palisades went even into the sea.

At Tagonoura waves were high. From there we
went along by boat. We went with ease over Nu-
majiri and came to the river Ōi. Such a torrent I
have never seen. Water, white as if thickened with
rice flour, ran fast.

I became ill, and now it is the Province of Tōtomi.
I had almost lost consciousness when I crossed the
mountain pass of Sayo-no-Nakayama [the middle
mountain of the little night]. I was quite exhausted,
so when we came to the bank of the Tenryu River,
we had a temporary dwelling built, and passed several
days there, and I got better. As the winter was

already advanced, the wind from the river blew hard
and it became intolerable. After crossing the river
we went towards the bridge at Hamana.

When we had gone down towards the East [four
years before when her father had been appointed
Governor] there had been a log bridge, but this
time we could not find even a trace of it, so we had
to cross in a boat. The bridge had been laid across an
inland bay. The waves of the outer sea were very
high, and we could see them through the thick pine-
trees which grew scattered over the sandy point
which stretched between us and the sea. They seemed
to strike across the ends of the pine branches and
shone like jewels. It was an interesting sight.

We went forward and crossed over Inohana—an
unspeakably weary ascent it was—and then came
to Takashi shore of the Province of Mikawa. We
passed a place called "Eight-Bridges," but it was
only a name, no bridge and no pretty sight.

In the mountain of Futamura we made our camp
under a big persimmon tree. The fruit fell down
during the night over our camps and people picked
it up.

We passed Mount Miyaji, where we saw red leaves
still, although it was the first day of the Tenth month.

Furious mountain winds in their passing
must spare this spot
For red maple leaves are clinging
even yet to the branch.

There was a fort of "If-I-can" between Mikawa

and Owari. It is amusing to think how difficult the crossing was, indeed. We passed the Narumi [sounding-sea] shore in the Province of Owari. The evening tides were coming in, and we thought if they came higher we could not cross. So in a panic we ran as fast as we could.

At the border of Mino we crossed a ferry called Kuromata, and arrived at Nogami. There singers came again and they sang all night. Lovingly we thought of the singers of Ashigara.

Snow came, and in the storm we passed the barrier at Fuha, and over the Mount Atsumi, having no heart to look at beautiful sights. In the Province of Omi we stayed four or five days in a house at Okinaga. At the foot of Mitsusaka Mountain light rain fell night and day mixed with hail. It was so melancholy that we left there and passed by Inugami, Kanzaki, and Yasu without receiving any impressions. The lake stretched far and wide, and we caught occasional glimpses of Nadeshima and Chikubushima [islands]. It was a very pretty sight. We had great difficulty at the bridge of Seta, for it had fallen in. We stopped at Awazu, and arrived at the Royal City after dark on the second day of the Finishing month.

When we were near the barrier I saw the face of a roughly hewn Buddha sixteen feet high which towered over a rude fence. Serene and indifferent to its surroundings it stood unregarded in this deserted place ; but I, passing by, received a message from it. Among so many provinces [through which I have passed] the barriers at Kiyomigata and Ōsaka were far better than the others.

It was dark when I arrived at the residence on the west of the Princess of Sanjo's mansion.[1] Our garden was very wide and wild with great, fearful trees not inferior to those mountains I had come from. I could not feel at home, or keep a settled mind. Even then I teased mother into giving me books of stories, after which I had been yearning for so many years. Mother sent a messenger with a letter to Emon-no-Myobu, one of our relatives who served the Princess of Sanjō. She took interest in my strange passion and willingly sent me some excellent manuscripts in the lid of a writing-box,[2] saying that these copies had been given her by the Princess. My joy knew no bounds and I read them day and night; I soon began to wish for more, but as I was an utter stranger to the Royal City, who would get them for me?

My stepmother [meaning one of her father's wives] had once been a lady-in-waiting at the court, and she seemed to have been disappointed in something. She had been regretting the World [her marriage], and now she was to leave our home. She beckoned her own child, who was five years old, and said, " The time will never come when I shall forget you, dear heart "; and pointing to a huge plum-tree which grew close to the eaves, said, " When it is in flower I

[1] The Princess was Sadako, daughter of King Sanjō, afterwards Queen of King Goshujaku (1037-1045).

[2] Lacquered boxes, sometimes of great beauty, containing india ink and inkstone, brushes, rolls of paper.

16

"IT WAS ALL IN FLOWER AND YET NO
TIDINGS FROM HER"

shall come back "; and she went away. I felt love and pity for her, and while I was secretly weeping, the year, too, went away.

" When the plum-tree blooms I shall come back " —I pondered over these words and wondered whether it would be so. I waited and waited with my eye hung to the tree. It was all in flower[1] and yet no tidings from her. I became very anxious [and at last] broke a branch and sent it to her [of course with a poem] :

You gave me words of hope, are they not long delayed?
The plum-tree is remembered by the Spring,
Though it seemed dead with frost.

She wrote back affectionate words with a poem :

Wait on, never forsake your hope,
For when the plum-tree is in flower
Even the unpromised, the unexpected, will come to you.

During the spring [of 1022] the world was dis-quieted.[2] My nurse, who had filled my heart with pity on that moonlight night at the ford of Matsu-zato, died on the moon-birthday of the Ever-growing month [first day of March]. I lamented hopelessly without any way to set my mind at ease, and even forgot my passion for romances.

I passed day after day weeping bitterly, and when

---

[1] Plum-trees bloom between the first and second months of the old calendar.

[2] By pestilence. People were often attacked by contagious diseases in those days, and they, who did not know about the nature of infection, called it by the name of " world-humor " or " world-disease," attributing its cause to the ill-humor of some gods or spirits.

17

I first looked out of doors[1] [again] I saw the evening sun on cherry-blossoms all falling in confusion [this would mean four weeks later].

Flowers are falling, yet I may see them again
when Spring returns.
But, oh, my longing for the dear person
who has departed from us forever!

I also heard that the daughter of the First Adviser[2] to the King was lost [dead]. I could sympathize deeply with the sorrow of her lord, the Lieutenant-General, for I still felt my own sorrow.

When I had first arrived at the Capital I had been given a book of the handwriting of this noble lady for my copy-book. In it were written several poems, among them the following :

When you see the smoke floating up the valley of
Toribe Hill,[3]
Then you will understand me, who seemed as shadow-like
even while living.

I looked at these poems which were written in such a beautiful handwriting, and I shed more tears. I sat brooding until mother troubled herself to console me. I became consoled unconsciously. I read a few volumes of Genji-monogatari and longed for the rest, but as I was still a stranger here I had no way of finding them. I was all impatience and yearning, and in my mind was always praying that I might read all the books of Genji-monogatari from the very first one.

[1] In those days windows were covered with silk and could not be seen through.
[2] Fujiwara-no-Yukinari: One of the three famous calligraphers of that
[3] Place where cremation was performed. [time.

Of Old Japan

While my parents were shutting themselves up in Udzu-Masa[1] Temple, I asked them for nothing except this romance, wishing to read it as soon as I could get it, but all in vain. I was inconsolable. One day I visited my aunt, who had recently come up from the country. She showed a tender interest in me and lovingly said I had grown up beautifully. On my return she said: " What shall I give you? You will not be interested in serious things: I will give you what you like best." And she gave me more than fifty volumes of Genji-monogatari put in a case, as well as Isé-monogatari, Togimi, Serikawa, Shirara, and Asa-udzu.[2] How happy I was when I came home carrying these books in a bag! Until then I had only read a volume here and there, and was dissatisfied because I could not understand the story.

Now I could be absorbed in these stories, taking them out one by one, shutting myself in behind the kichō.[3] To be a Queen were nothing compared to this!

All day and all night, as late as I could keep my eyes open, I did nothing but look at the books, setting a lamp[4] close beside me.

Soon I learnt by heart all the names in the books, and I thought that a great thing.

Once I dreamt of a holy priest in yellow Buddhist scarf who came to me and said, "Learn the fifth book of the Hokekkyo[5] at once."

---

[1] It is a Buddhist custom to go into retreat from time to time.
[2] Some of these books are not known now.
[3] A kind of screen used in upper-class houses: see illustration.
[4] Her lamp was rather like an Italian one—a shallow cup for oil fixed to a tall metal stem, with a wick projecting to one side.
[5] Sadharmpundarika Sutra, or Sutra of the Lotus, in Sanscrit.

I did not tell any one about this, nor had I any mind to learn it, but continued to bathe in the romances. Although I was still ugly and undeveloped [I thought to myself] the time would come when I should be beautiful beyond compare, with long, long hair. I should be like the Lady Yugao [in the romance] loved by the Shining Prince Genji, or like the Lady Ukifuné, the wife of the General of Uji [a famous beauty]. I indulged in such fancies—shallow-minded I was, indeed!

Could such a man as the Shining Prince be living in this world? How could General Kaoru [literal translation, "Fragrance"] find such a beauty as the Lady Ukifuné to conceal in his secret villa at Uji? Oh! I was like a crazy girl.

While I had lived in the country, I had gone to the temple from time to time, but even then I could never pray like others, with a pure heart. In those days people learned to recite sutras and practise austerities of religious observance after the age of seventeen or eighteen, but I could scarcely even think of such matters. The only thing that I could think of was the Shining Prince who would some day come to me, as noble and beautiful as in the romance. If he came only once a year I, being hidden in a mountain villa like the Lady Ukifuné, would be content. I could live as *heart-dwindlingly* as that lady, looking at flowers, or moonlit snowy landscape, occasionally receiving long-expected lovely letters from my Lord! I cherished such fancies and imagined that they might be realized.

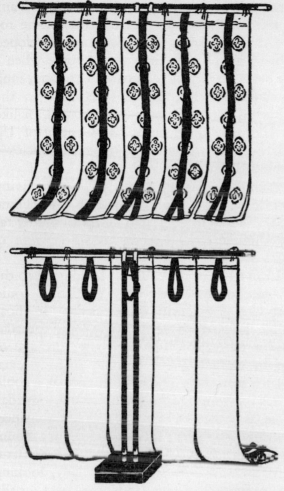

KICHŌ: FRONT AND BACK VIEWS

Of Old Japan

On the moon-birth of the Rice-Sprout month I saw the white petals of the Tachibana tree [a kind of orange] near the house covering the ground.

> *Scarce had my mind received with wonder*
> *The thought of newly fallen snow—*
> *Seeing the ground lie white—*
> *When the scent of Tachibana flowers*
> *Arose from fallen blossoms.*

In our garden trees grew as thick as in the dark forest of Ashigara, and in the Gods-absent month[1] its red leaves were more beautiful than those of the surrounding mountains. A visitor said, " On my way thither I passed a place where red leaves were beautiful "; and I improvised :

> *No sight can be more autumnal*
> *than that of my garden*
> *Tenanted by an autumnal person*
> *weary of the world!*

I still dwelt in the romances from morning to night, and as long as I was awake.

I had another dream : a man said that he was to make a brook in the garden of the Hexagon Tower to entertain the Empress of the First Rank of Honour. I asked the reason, and the man said, " Pray to the Heaven-illuminating honoured Goddess." I did not tell any one about this dream or even think of it again. How shallow I was !

[1] In October it was the custom for all local gods to go for a conference to the residence of the oldest native god, in the Province of Izumo ; hence, *Gods-absent month*. This Province of Idzumo, full of the folklore of old Japan, has become well known to the world through the writings of Lafcadio Hearn.

21

In the Spring I enjoyed the Princess's garden. Cherry-blossoms waited for!—cherry-blossoms lamented over! In Spring I love the flowers whether in her garden or in mine.

On the moon-hidden day of the Ever-growing month [March 30, 1023], I started for a certain person's house to avoid the evil influence of the earth god.[1] There I saw delightful cherry-blossoms still on the tree and the day after my return I sent this poem :

Alone, without tiring, I gazed at the cherry-blossoms of your garden.
The Spring was closing—they were about to fall—

Always when the flowers came and went, I could think of nothing but those days when my nurse died, and sadness descended upon me, which grew deeper when I studied the handwriting of the Honoured Daughter of the First Adviser.

Once in the Rice-Sprout month, when I was up late reading a romance, I heard a cat mewing with a long-drawn-out cry. I turned, wondering, and saw a very lovely cat. " Whence does it come?" I asked. " Sh," said my sister, " do not tell anybody. It is a darling cat and we will keep it."

The cat was very sociable and lay beside us. Some one might be looking for her [we thought], so we kept her secretly. She kept herself aloof from the vulgar

[1] According to the superstition of those days people believed that every house was presided over by an earth god, which occupied the hearth in Spring, the gate in Summer, the well in Autumn, and the garden in Winter. It was dangerous to meet him when he changed his abode. So on that day the dwellers went out from their houses.

servants, always sitting quietly before us. She turned her face away from unclean food, never eating it. She was tenderly cared for and caressed by us.

Once sister was ill, and the family was rather upset. The cat was kept in a room facing the north [i.e. a servant's room], and never was called. She cried loudly and scoldingly, yet I thought it better to keep her away and did so. Sister, suddenly awakening, said to me, " Where is the cat kept? Bring her here." I asked why, and sister said : " In my dream the cat came to my side and said, ' I am the altered form of the late Honoured Daughter of the First Adviser to the King. There was a slight cause (for this). Your sister has been thinking of me affectionately, so I am here for a while, but now I am among the servants. O how dreary I am!' So saying she wept bitterly. She appeared to be a noble and beautiful person and then I awoke to hear the cat crying! How pitiful!"

The story moved me deeply and after this I never sent the cat away to the north-facing room, but waited on her lovingly. Once, when I was sitting alone, she came and sat before me, and, stroking her head, I addressed her : " You are the first daughter of the Noble Adviser? I wish to let your father know of it." The cat watched my face and mewed, *lengthening her voice.*

It may be my fancy, but as I was watching her she seemed no common cat. She seemed to understand my words, and I pity her.

I had heard that a certain person possessed the

23

Chogonka [Song of the Long Regret] retold from the original of the Chinese poet Li T'ai Po. I longed to borrow it, but was too shy to say so.

On the seventh day of the Seventh month I found a happy means to send my word [the suggestion of my wish] :

> *This is the night when in the ancient Past,*
> *The Herder Star embarked to meet the Weaving One;*[1]
> *In its sweet remembrance the wave rises high in the River*
> *of Heaven.*[2]
> *Even ao swells my heart to see the famous book.*

The answer was :

> *The star gods meet on the shore of the Heavenly River,*
> *Like theirs full of ecstacy is my heart*

[1] Readers are urged to read the delightful essay of Lafcadio Hearn called " The Romance of the Milky Way." Here it must suffice to relate the story of " Tanabata-himé " and the herdsman. Tanabata-tsumé was the daughter of the god of the sky. She rejoiced to weave garments for her father and had no greater pleasure than that, until one day Hikoboshi, a young herdsman, leading an ox, passed by her door. Divining her love for him, her father gave his daughter the young herdsman for her husband, and all went well, until the young couple grew too fond of each other and the weaving was neglected. Thereupon the great god was displeased and " they were sentenced to live apart with the Celestial River between them," but in pity of their love they were permitted to meet one night a year, on the seventh day of the Seventh month. On that night the herdsman crosses the River of Heaven where Tanabata-tsumé is waiting for him on the other side, but woe betide if the night is cloudy or rainy. Then the waters of the River of Heaven rise, and the lovers must wait full another year before the boat can cross.

Many of our beautiful poems have been written on this legend ; sometimes it is Tanabata-himé who is waiting for her lord, sometimes it is Hikoboshi who speaks. The festival has been celebrated for 1100 years in Japan, and there is no country village which does not sing these songs on the seventh night of the Seventh month, and make offerings to the star gods of little poems tied to freshly cut bamboo branches.

[2] River of Heaven : Milky Way.

24

Of Old Japan

And grave things of daily life are forgotten
On the night your message comes to me.

On the thirteenth day of that month the moon shone very brightly. Darkness was chased away even from every corner of the heavens. It was about midnight and all were asleep.

We were sitting on the veranda. My sister, who was gazing at the sky thoughtfully, said, " If I flew away now, leaving no trace behind, what would you think of it ?" She saw that her words shocked me, and she turned the conversation [lightly] to other things, and we laughed.

Then I heard a carriage with a runner before it stop near the house. The man in the carriage called out, " Ogi-no-ha ! Ogi-no-ha ! " [Reed-leaf, a woman's name or pet name] twice, but no woman made reply. The man cried in vain until he was tired of it, and played his flute [a reed-pipe] more and more searchingly in a very beautiful rippling melody, and [at last] drove away.

Flute music in the night,
" Autumn Wind "[1] sighing,
Why does the reed-leaf make no reply ?

Thus I challenged my sister, and she took it up :

Alas ! light of heart
Who could so soon give over playing !
The wind did not wait,
For the response of the reed-leaf.

We sat together looking up into the firmament, and went to bed after daybreak.

[1] Name of an old song.

At midnight of the Deutzia month [April, 1024] a fire broke out, and the cat which had been waited on as a daughter of the First Adviser was burned to death. She had been used to come mewing whenever I called her by the name of that lady, as if she had understood me. My father said that he would tell the matter to the First Adviser, for it is a strange and heartfelt story. I was very, very sorry for her.

Our new temporary shelter was far narrower than the other. I was sad, for we had a very small garden and no trees. I thought with regret of the old spacious garden which was wild as a deep wood, and in time of flowers and red leaves the sight of it was never inferior to the surrounding mountains.

In the garden of the opposite house white and red plum-blossoms grew in confusion and their perfume came on the wind and filled me with thoughts of our old home.

When from the neighbouring garden the perfume-laden air
Saturates my soul with memories,
Rises the thought of the beloved plum-tree
Blooming under the eaves of the house which is gone.

On the moon-birth of the Rice-Sprout month my sister died after giving birth to a child. From childhood, even a stranger's death had touched my heart deeply. This time I lamented, filled with speechless pity and sorrow.

While mother and the others were with the dead, I lay with the memory-awakening children one on either side of me. The moonlight found its way through the cracks of the roof [perhaps of their tem-

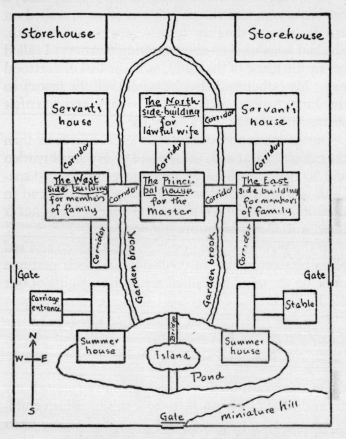

Storehouse Storehouse

Servant's house

The North-side-building for lawful wife

Corridor

Servant's house

Corridor Corridor Corridor

The West side-building for members of family

Corridor

The Principal house, for the Master

Corridor

The East side-building for members of family

Corridor Corridor

Garden brook Garden brook

Gate Gate

Carriage entrance Stable

N
W E
S

Summer house

Bridge

Island

Summer house

Pond

Gate miniature hill

A NOBLEMAN'S HOUSE AND GROUNDS
IN THE AZUMAYA STYLE

porary dwelling] and illumined the face of the baby. The sight gave my heart so deep a pang that I covered its face with my sleeve, and drew the other child closer to my side, mothering the unfortunate.

After some days one of my relatives sent me a romance entitled " The Prince Yearning after the Buried," with the following note : " The late lady had asked me to find her this romance. At that time I thought it impossible, but now to add to my sorrow, some one has just sent it to me."

I answered :

> *What reason can there be that she*
> *Strangely should seek a romance of the buried?*
> *Buried now is the seeker*
> *Deep under the mosses.*

My sister's nurse said that since she had lost her, she had no reason to stay and went back to her own home weeping.

> *Thus death or parting separates us each from the other,*
> *Why must we part? Oh, world too sad for me!*

" For remembrance of her I wanted to write about her," began a letter from her nurse—but it stopped short with the words, " Ink seems to have frozen up, I cannot write any more." [1]

> *How shall I gather memories of my sister?*
> *The stream of letter is congealed.*
> *No comfort may be found in icicles.*

[1] The continuous writing of the cursive Japanese characters is often compared to a meandering river. " Ink seems to have frozen up " means that her eyes are dim with tears, and no more she can write continuously and flowingly.

27

So I wrote, and the answer was :

Like the comfortless plover of the beach
In the sand printing characters soon to be washed away,
Unable to leave a more enduring trace in this fleeting world.

That nurse went to see the grave and returned sobbing, saying :

I seek her in the field, but she is not there,
Nor is she in the smoke of the cremation.
Where is her last dwelling-place ?
How can I find it ?

The lady who had been my stepmother heard of this [and wrote]:

When we wander in search of her,
Ignorant of her last dwelling-place,
Standing before the thought
Tears must be our guide.

The person who had sent " The Prince Yearning after the Buried " wrote :

How she must have wandered seeking the unfindable
In the unfamiliar fields of bamboo grasses,
Vainly weeping!

Reading these poems my brother, who had followed the funeral that night, composed a poem :

Before my vision
The fire and smoke of burning
Arose and died again.
To bamboo fields there is no more returning,
Why seek there in vain ?

It snowed for many days, and I thought of the nun who lived on Mount Yoshino, to whom I wrote :

28

Of Old Japan

Snow has fallen
And you cannot have
Even the unusual sight of men
Along the precipitous path of the Peak of Yoshino.

On the Sociable month of the next year father was looking forward with happy expectation to the night when he might expect an appointment as Governor of a Province. He was disappointed, and a person who might have shared our joy wrote to me, saying :

" I anxiously waited for the dawn with uncertain hope."

The temple bell roused me from dreams
And waiting for the starlit dawn
The night, alas! was long as are
One hundred autumn nights.

I wrote back :

Long was the night.
The bell called from dreams in vain,
For it did not toll our realized hopes.

Towards the moon-hidden days [last days] of the Rice-Sprout month I went for a certain reason to a temple at Higashiyama.[1] On the way the nursery beds for rice-plants were filled with water, and the fields were green all over with the young growing rice. It was a smile-presenting sight. It gave a feeling of loneliness to see the dark shadow of the mountain close before me. In the lovely evenings water-rails chattered in the fields.

The water-rails cackle as if they were knocking at the gate,
But who would be deceived into opening the door, saying,
Our friend has come along the mountain path in the dark night?

[1] A mountain in a suburb of Kyoto.

As the place was near the Reizan Temple I went there
to worship. Arriving so far I was fatigued, and
drank from a stone-lined well beside the mountain
temple, scooping the water into the hollow of my
hand.

My friend said, " I could never have enough of this
water." "Is it the first time," I asked, " that you have
tasted the satisfying sweetness of a mountain well
drunk from the hollow of your hand ?" She said,
" It is sweeter than to drink from a shallow spring,
which becomes muddy even from the drops which fall
from the hand which has scooped it up."[1] We came
home from the temple in the full brightness of evening sunshine, and had a clear view of Kyoto below
us.

My friend, who had said that a spring becomes
muddy even with drops falling into it, had to go back
to the Capital.

I was sorry to part with her and sent word the next
morning :

> *When the evening sun descends behind the mountain peak,*
> *Will you forget that it is I who gaze with longing*
> *Towards the place where you are ?*

The holy voices of the priests reciting sutras in
their morning service could be heard from my house
and I opened the door. It was dim early dawn ; mist
veiled the green forest, which was thicker and darker
than in the time of flowers or red leaves. The sky

---

[1] This conversation in the original is a play upon words which cannot be
translated.

seemed clouded this lovely morning. Cuckoos were singing on the near-by trees.

> O for a friend—that we might see and listen together!
> O the beautiful dawn in the mountain village!—
> The repeated sound of cuckoos near and far away.

On that moon-hidden day cuckoos sung clamorously on trees towards the glen. " In the Royal City poets may be awaiting you, cuckoos, yet you sing here carelessly from morning till night ! "

One who sat near me said : " Do you think that there is one person, at least, in the Capital who is listening to cuckoos, and thinking of us at this moment ? "—and then :

> Many in the Royal City like to gaze on the calm moon.
> But is there one who thinks of the deep mountain
> Or is reminded of us hidden here?

I replied :

> In the dead of night, moon-gazing,
> The thought of the deep mountain affrighted,
> Yet longings for the mountain village
> At all other moments filled my heart.

Once, towards dawn, I heard footsteps which seemed to be those of many persons coming down the mountain. I wondered and looked out. It was a herd of deer which came close to our dwelling. They cried out. It was not pleasant to hear them near by.

> It is sweet to hear the love-call of a deer to its mate,
> In Autumn nights, upon the distant hills.

I heard that an acquaintance had come near my

residence and gone back without calling on me. So I wrote :

Even this wandering wind among the pines of the mountain—
I've heard that it departs with murmuring sound.

[That is, you are not like it. You do not speak when going away.]

In the Leaf-Falling month [September] I saw the moon more than twenty days old. It was towards dawn ; the mountain-side was gloomy and the sound of the waterfall was all [I heard]. I wish that lovers [of nature] may see the after-dawn-waning moon in a mountain village at the close of an autumn night.

I went back to Kyoto when the rice-fields, which had been filled with water when I came, were dried up, the rice being harvested. The young plants in their bed of water—the plants harvested—the fields dried up—so long I remained away from home.

'T was the moon-hidden of the Gods-absent month when I went there again for temporary residence. The thick grown leaves which had cast a dark shade were all fallen. The sight was heartfelt over all. The sweet, murmuring rivulet was buried under fallen leaves and I cound see only the course of it.

Even water could not live on—
So lonesome is the mountain
Of the leaf-scattering stormy wind.

[At about this time the author of this diary seems to have had some family troubles. Her father received no appointment from the King—they were probably poor, and her gentle, poetic nature did

32

not incline her to seek useful friends at court; therefore many of the best years of her youth were spent in obscurity—a great contrast to the "Shining-Prince" dreams of her childhood.]

I went back to Kioto saying that I should come again the next Spring, could I live so long, and begged the nun to send word when the flowering-time had come.

It was past the nineteenth of the Ever-growing month of the next year [1026], but there were no tidings from her, so I wrote :

No word about the blooming cherry-blossoms,
Has not the Spring come for you yet ?
Or does the perfume of flowers not reach you ?

I made a journey, and passed many a moonlit night in a house beside a bamboo wood. Wind rustled its leaves and my sleep was disturbed.

Night after night the bamboo leaves sigh,
My dreams are broken and a vague, indefinite sadness
fills my heart.

In Autumn [1026] I went to live elsewhere and sent a poem :

I am like dew on the grass—
And pitiable wherever I may be—
But especially am I oppressed with sadness
In a field with a thin growth of reeds.

After that time I was somehow restless and forgot about the romances. My mind became more sober and I passed many years without doing any remark-

33

able thing. I neglected religious services and temple observances. Those fantastic ideas [of the romances] can they be realized in this world ? If father could win some good position I also might enter into a much nobler life. Such unreliable hopes then occupied my daily thoughts.

At last[1] father was appointed Governor of a Province very far in the East.

[Here the diary skips six years. The following is reminiscent.]

He [father] said : " I was always thinking that if I could win a position as Governor in the neighbourhood of the Capital I could take care of you to my heart's desire. I would wish to bring you down to see beautiful scenery of sea and mountain. Moreover, I wished that you could live attended beyond [the possibilities] of our [present] position. Our Karma relation from our former world must have been bad. Now I have to go to so distant a country after waiting so long ! When I brought you, who were a little child, to the Eastern Province [at his former appointment], even a slight illness caused me much trouble of mind in thinking that should I die, you would wander helpless in that far country. There were many fears in a stranger's country, and I should have lived with an easier mind had I been alone. As I was then accompanied by all my family, I could not say or do what I wanted to say or do, and I was ashamed of it. Now you are grown up [she was

---

[1] In an old chronicle of the times one reads that it was on February 8, 1032.

twenty-five years old] and I am not sure that I can live long.

It is not so unusual a fate to be helpless in the Capital, but the saddest thing of all would be to wander in the Eastern Province like any country-woman.[1] There are no relatives in the Capital upon whom we could rely to foster you, yet I cannot refuse the appointment which has been made after such long waiting. So you must remain here, and I must depart for Eternity.—Oh, in what way can I provide a way for you to live in the Capital decently !

Night and day he lamented, saying these things, and I forgot all about flowers or maple leaves, grieving sadly, but there was no help for it.

He went down[2] on the thirteenth of the Seventh month, 1032.

For several days before that I could not remain still in my own room, for I thought it difficult to see him again.

On that day [the 13th] after restless hours, when the [time for] parting came, I had lifted the blind and my eye met his, from which tears dropped down. Soon he had passed by.[3] My eyes were dim with tears and

---

[1] The country people of the Eastern Provinces beyond Tokyo were then called "Eastern barbarians."

[2] Away from the Capital where the King resides is always *down*; towards the capital is always *up*.

[3] This scene will be better understood by the reader if he remembers that her father was in the street in the midst of his train of attendants—an imposing cavalcade of bow-men, warriors, and attendants of all sorts, with palanquins and luggage, prepared to make a two or three months' journey through the wilderness to the Province of Hitachi, far in the East. She, as a Japanese lady could not go out to speak to him, but unconventionally she had drawn up the blind and "her eye met his."

35

soon I concealed myself in bed [tears were bad manners]. A man who had gone to see him off returned with a poem written on a bit of pocket paper.

A message from her father :

> *If I could do as I wish*
> *I could acknowledge more profoundly*
> *The sorrow of departing in Autumn.*

[The last line has, of course, reference to his age and the probability of never returning.]

I could not read the poem to the end.

In the happier time I had often tried to compose halting poems [literally, of broken loins] but at present I had no word to say.

> *—never began to think in this world even for*
> *a moment from you to part. Alas!*

No person came to my side and I was very lonely and forlorn musing and guessing where he would be at every moment. As I knew the road he was taking [the same which is described in this journal], I thought of him the more longingly and with greater heart-shrinking. Morning and evening I looked towards the sky-line of the eastern mountains.

In the Leaf-Falling month I went to the temple at Udzumaza [Korinji] to pass many days.

We came upon two men's palanquins in the road from Ichijo, which had stopped there. They must have been waiting for some one to catch up with them. When I passed by they sent an attendant with the message : "Flower-seeing go ?—we suppose."

I thought it would be awkward not to reply to such a slight matter, and answered :

Thousand kinds[1]—
To be like them in the field of Autumn.

I stayed in the temple for seven days, but could think of nothing but the road to the East.

I prayed to the Buddha, saying : " There is no way to change the present, but grant that we may meet again peacefully after this parting "—and I thought the Buddha would pity and grant my prayer.

It was midwinter. It rained all day. In the night a cloud-turning wind blew terribly and the sky cleared. The moon became exquisitely bright, and it was sad to see the tall reeds near the house broken and blown down by the wind.

Dead stalks of reeds must be reminded of good Autumn days.
In midwinter depths the tempest lays them low,
Confused and broken.

" [Their fate is like my own," is intangibly expressed in this poem.]

A messenger arrived from the East.

Father's letter :

" I wandered through the Province [Hitachi, now Ibara-kiken] going into every Shinto shrine and saw a wide field with a beautiful river running through it.[2] There was a beautiful wood. My first thought was of you, and to make you see it, and I asked the name of that grove. 'The

[1] To translate : As there are a thousand kinds of flowers in the autumn fields, so there are a thousand reasons for going to the fields.
[2] The Toné River.

grove of Longing After One's Child ' was the answer. I
thought of the one who had first named it and was extremely sad. Alighting from my horse I stood there for two
hours.

After leaving—
Like me he must have yearned
Sorrowful to see—
The forest of Longing After One's Child."

To see that letter is a sadder thing than to have
seen the forest.

[The poem sent in return presents difficulties in the
way of translation as there is a play upon words,
literally it is something like this :]

The grove of "Longing After One's Child " ; left ;
Father-caressed[1] Mountain ; [Chichibusan] hard
Eastern way—

The grove of longing After One's Child—
Hearing of it I think of the Father-caressed Mountain :
Towards it hard is the Eastern way
For a child left [here alone].

Thus I passed days in doing nothing, and I began
to think of going to temples [making pilgrimages].
Mother was a person of extremely antiquated mind.
She said : " Oh, dreadful is the Hatsusé Temple !
What should you do if you were caught by some one
at the Nara ascent ? Ishiyama too ! Sekiyama Pass
[near Lake Biwa] is very dreadful ! Kurama-san [the
famous mountain], oh, dreadful to bring you there !
You may go there when father comes back."

[1] Name of mountain in eastern part of Japan.

38

As mother says so, I can go only to Kiyomidzu Temple.[1] My old habits of romantic indulgence were not dead yet, and I could not fix my mind on religious thoughts as I ought.

In the equinoctial week there was a great tumult [of festival], so great a noise that I was even afraid of it, and when I lay asleep I dreamt there was a priest within the enclosure before the altar, in blue garments with loose brocade hood and brocade shoes. He seemed to be the intendant of the temple : " You, being occupied with vain thoughts, are not praying for happiness in the world to come," he said indignantly, and went behind the curtain. I awoke startled, yet neither told any one what I had dreamt, nor thought about it much.

My mother had two one-foot-in-diameter bronze mirrors cast and made a priest take them for us to the Hatsusé Temple. Mother told the priest to pass two or three days in the temple especially praying that a dream might be vouchsafed about the future state of this woman [the daughter]. For that period I was made to observe religious purity [i.e. abstain from animal food.]

The priest came back to tell the following :

" I was reluctant to return without having even a dream, and after bowing many times and performing other ceremonies I went to sleep. There came out from behind the curtain a graceful holy lady in beautiful garments. She, taking up the offered mirrors,

---

[1] In the eastern part of Kyoto, now a famous spot.

asked me if no letters were affixed to these mirrors. I answered in the most respectful manner, ' There were no letters. I was told only to offer these.' ' Strange !' she said. ' Letters are to be added. See what is mirrored in one, it creates pity to look at it.' I saw her weep bitterly and saw appear in the mirror shadows of people rolling over in lamentation. 'To see these shadows makes one sad, but to see this makes one happy,' and she held up the other mirror. There, the *misu* was fresh green and many-coloured garments were revealed below the lower edge of it. Plum and cherry-blossoms were in flower. Nightingales were singing from tree to tree."

I did not even listen to his story nor question him as to how things seemed in his dream. Some one said, " Pray to the Heaven Illuminating Honoured Goddess," and my irreverent mind thought, "Where is she ? Is she a Goddess or a Buddha ?"

At first I said so, but afterwards grew more discreet and asked some one about her, who replied : " She is a goddess, and takes up her abode at Isé.[1] The goddess is also worshipped by the Provincial Governor of Kii. She is worshipped at the ancestor shrine in the Imperial Court."

I could not by any means get to Isé. How could I bow before the Imperial shrine ? I could never be allowed to go there. The idea flowed through my mind to pray for the heavenly light.

[1] The Isé shrine was first built in the year 3 B.C. See note on Isé shrine in Murasaki Shikibu Diary.

A relative of mine became a nun, and entered the Sugaku Temple. In winter I sent her a poem:

> *Even tears arise for your sake*
> *When I think of the mountain hamlet*
> *Where snow-storms will be raging.*

Reply:

> *I seem to have a glimpse of you*
> *Coming to me through the dark wood,*
> *When close overhead is Summer's growth of leaves.*

1036. Father, who had gone down towards the East, came back at last. He settled down at Nishiyama, and we all went there. We were very happy. One moon-bright night we talked all the night through:

> *Such nights as this exist!*
> *As if it were for Eternity, I parted from you—*
> *How sad was that Autumn!*

At this father shed tears [of happiness] abundantly, and answered me with a poem:

> *That life grows dear and is lived with rejoicing*
> *Which once was borne with hate and lamentation.*

My joy knew no bounds when my waiting was at an end after the supposed parting "for Eternity," yet my father said: "It is ridiculous to lead a worldly life when one is very old. I used to feel so when I saw old men, but now it is my turn to be old, so I will retire from social life." As he said it with no lingering affection for this world, I felt quite alone.

Towards the East the field stretched far and wide

and I could see clearly from Mount Hiyé[1] to Mount Inari. Towards the West, the pines of the forest of Narabigaoka were sounding in my ear, and up to the tableland on which our house stood the rice-fields were cultivated in terraces, while from them came the sound of the bird-scaring clappers, giving me a homely country sentiment.

One moonlight evening I had a message from an old acquaintance who had had an opportunity to send to me, and this I sent back :

None calls upon me, or remembers me in my mountain village.
On the reeds by the thin hedge, the Autumn winds are sighing.

1037. In the Tenth month we changed our abode to the Capital. Mother had become a nun, and although she lived in the same house, shut herself up in a separate chamber. Father rather treated me as an independent woman than as his child. I felt helpless to see him shunning all society and living hidden in the shade.

A person [the Princess Yûko, daughter of the Emperor Goshujaku] who had heard about me through a distant relative called me [to her] saying it would be better [to be with her] than passing idle lonely days.

My old-fashioned parents thought the court life would be very unpleasant, and wanted me to pass my time at home, but others said : " People nowadays go out as ladies-in-waiting at the Court, and then fortunate opportunities [for marriage] are naturally

---

[1] Mt. Hiyé : 2500 ft. toward the north-east of Kyoto.

numerous ; why not try it ?" So [at the age of twenty-six] I was sent to the Court against my will.

I went for one night the first time. I was dressed in an eight-fold uchigi of deep and pale chrysanthemum colors, and over it I wore the outer flowing robe of deep-red silk.

As I have said before, my mind was absorbed in romances, and I had no important relatives from whom I could learn distinguished manners or court customs, so except from the romances I could not know them. I had always been in the shadow of the antiquated parents, and had been accustomed not to go out but to see moon and flowers. So when I left home I felt as if I were not I nor was it the real world [to which I was going]. I started in the early morning. I had often fancied in my countrified mind that I should hear more interesting things for my heart's consolation than were to be found living fixed in my parents' house.

I felt awkward in Court in everything I did, and I thought it sad, but there was no use in complaining. I remembered with grief my nieces who had lost their mother and had been cared for by me alone, even sleeping at night one on either side of me.

Days were spent in musing with a vacant mind. I felt as if some one were [always] spying upon me, and I was embarrassed.[1] After ten days or so I got leave

---

[1] The custom of the Court obliged the court ladies to lead a life of almost no privacy—sleeping at night together in the presence of the Queen, and sharing their apartments with each other.

to go out. Father and mother were waiting for me with a comfortable fire in a brazier.

Seeing me getting out of my palanquin, my nieces said : " When you were with us people came to see us, but now no one's voice is heard, no one's shadow falls before the house. We are very low-spirited ; what can you do for us who must pass days like this ?" It was pitiful to see them cry when they said it. The next morning they sat before me, saying : " As you are here many persons are coming and going. It seems livelier."

Tears came to my eyes to think what virtue [literally, fragrance] I could have that my little nieces made so much of me.

It would be very difficult even for a saint to dream of his prenatal life. Yet, when I was before the altar of the Kiyomidzu Temple, in a faintly dreamy state of mind which was neither sleeping nor waking, I saw a man who seemed to be the head of the temple. He came out and said to me :

" You were once a priest of this temple and you were born into a better state by virtue of the many Buddhist images which you carved as a Buddhist artist. The Buddha seventeen feet high which is enthroned in the eastern side of the temple was your work. When you were in the act of covering it with gold foil you died."

" Oh, undeservedly blessed !" I said. " I will finish it, then."

The priest replied : " As you died, another man covered it and performed the ceremony of offerings."

44

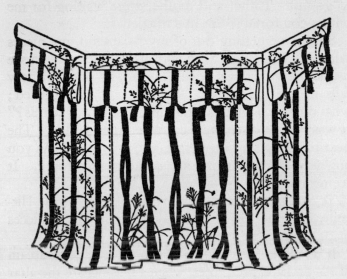

THREE KICHŌ PUT TOGETHER

The curtains of the screen, or kichō, varied with the seasons.
This is a summer one with decorations of
summer grasses and flowers.

I came to myself and thought : " If I serve with all my heart the Buddha of the Kiyomidzu Temple . . . by virtue of my prayers in this temple in the previous life . . ."[1]

In the Finishing month I went again to the Court. A room was assigned for my use.

I went to the Princess's apartment every night and lay down among unknown persons, so I could not sleep at all. I was bashful and timid and wept in secret. In the morning I retired while it was still dark and passed the days in longing for home where my old and weak parents, making much of me, relied upon me as if I were worthy of it. I yearned for them and felt very lonely. Unfortunate, deplorable, and helpless mind !—That was graven into my thought and although I had to perform my duty faithfully I could not always wait upon the Princess. She seemed not to guess what was in my heart, and attributing it only to shyness favored me by summoning me often from among the other ladies. She used to say, " Call the younger ladies ! " and I was dragged out in spite of myself.

Those who were familiar with the court life seemed to be at home there, but I, who was not very young, yet did not wish to be counted among the elderly, was rather neglected, and made to usher guests. However, I did not expect too much of court life, and had no envy for those who were more graceful than I. This, on the contrary, set me at ease, and I from time

---

[1] Some words are lost from this sentence.

to time presented myself before the Princess ; and talked only with congenial friends about lovely things. Even on smile-presenting, interesting occasions I shrank from intruding and becoming too popular, and did not go far into most things.

Sleeping one night before the Princess, I was awakened by cries and fluttering noises from the waterfowl in the pond.

> *Like us the waterfowl pass all the night in floating sleep,*
> *They seem to be weary*
> *With shaking away the frost from their feathers.*

My companions passed their leisure time in talking over romances with the door open which separated our rooms, and they often called back one who had gone to the Princess's apartment. She sent word once, " I will go if I must " [intending to give herself the pleasure of coming.]

> *The long leaves of the reed are easily bent,*
> *So I will not forcibly persuade it,*
> *But leave it to the wind.*

In this way [composing poems] we passed [the hours] talking idly. Afterwards this lady separated from the Court and left us. She remembered that night and sent me word—

> *That moonless, flowerless winter night*
> *It penetrates my thought and makes me dwell on it—*
> *   I wonder why?*

It touched my heart, for I also was thinking of that night :

46

In my dreams the tears of that cold night are still frozen.
But these I weep away secretly.

The Princess still called my stepmother by the name
of Kazusa[1]—Governor's lady. Father was displeased that that name was still used after she had
become another man's wife, and he made me write to
her about it :

The name of Asakura in a far-off country,
The Court now hears it in a divine dance-song:—
My name also is still somewhere heard [but not honourably].[2]

One very bright night, after the full moon, I attended the Princess to the Imperial Palace. I remembered that the Heaven Illuminating Goddess was
enthroned within, and wanted to take an opportunity to kneel before the altar. One moon-bright night
[1042 A.D.] I went in [to the shrine] privately, for I
know Lady Hakasé[3] who was taking care of this
shrine. The perpetual lights before the altar burned
dimly. She [the Lady Hakasé] grew wondrously old
and holy ; she seems not like a mortal, but like a
divine incarnation, yet she spoke very gracefully.

The moon was very bright on the following night
and the Princess's ladies passed the time in talking
and moon-gazing, opening the doors [outer shutters]
of the Fujitsubo.[4] The footsteps of the Royal consort

---

[1] Kazusa : Name of Province in the East.
[2] Asakura is a place-name in Kyushu. There was a song entitled " Asakura " which seems to have been popular in those days and was sung in the
Court.
[3] Hakasé is LL.D., so she might have been daughter of a scholar.
[4] Special house devoted to use of a Queen.

of Umetsubo going up to the King's apartment were so exquisitely graceful as to excite envy. " Had the late Queen[1] been living, she could not walk so grandly," some one said. I composed a poem :

She is like the Moon, who, opening the gate of Heaven,
goes up over the clouds.
We, being in the same heavenly Palace, pass the night
in remembering the footfalls of the past.

The ladies who are charged with the duty of introducing the court nobles seem to have been fixed upon, and nobody notices whether simple-hearted country-women like me exist or not. On a very dark night in the beginning of the Gods-absent month, when sweet-voiced reciters were to read sutras throughout the night, another lady and I went out towards the entrance door of the Audience Room to listen to it, and after talking fell asleep, listening, leaning, . . .[2] when I noticed a gentleman had come to be received in audience by the Princess.

" It is awkward to run away to our apartment [to escape him]. We will remain here. Let it be as it will." So said my companion and I sat beside her listening.

He spoke gently and quietly. There was nothing about him to be regretted. "Who is the other lady?" he asked of my friend. He said nothing rude or amorous like other men, but talked delicately of the sad,

[1] The Princess, whom our lady served, was the daughter of King Goshujaku's Queen. The Queen died 1039. After this the Royal Consort Umetsubo won the King's favour.
[2] Some words lost.

48

sweet things of the world, and many a phrase of his with a strange power enticed me into conversation. He wondered that there should have been in the Court one who was a stranger to him, and did not seem inclined to go away soon.

There was no starlight, and a gentle shower fell in the darkness; how lovely was its sound on the leaves! " The more deeply beautiful is the night," he said ; " the full moonlight would be too dazzling." Discoursing about the beauties of Spring and Autumn he continued : " Although every hour has its charm, pretty is the spring haze ; then the sky being tranquil and overcast, the face of the moon is not too bright ; it seems to be floating on a distant river. At such a time the calm spring melody of the lute is exquisite.

" In Autumn, on the other hand, the moon is very bright ; though there are mists trailing over the horizon we can see things as clearly as if they were at hand. The sound of wind, the voices of insects, all sweet things seem to melt together. When at such a time we listen to the autumnal music of the koto[1] we forget the Spring—we think that is best—

" But the winter sky frozen all over magnificently cold ! The snow covering the earth and its light mingling with the moonshine ! Then the notes of the hitchiriki[2] vibrate on the air and we forget Spring and Autumn." And he asked us, " Which captivates your fancy ? On which stays your mind ?"

---

[1] A thirteen-stringed musical instrument.

[2] A pipe made of seven reeds having a very clear, piercing sound.

My companion answered in favour of Autumn and I, not being willing to imitate her, said :

*Pale green buds and flowers all melting into one
in the soft haze—
Faintly glimmers the moon in the Spring night.*

So I replied. And he, after repeating my poem to himself over and over, said : " Then you give up Autumn ? After this, as long as I live, such a spring night shall be for me a memento of your personality." The person who favoured Autumn said, " Others seem to give their hearts to Spring, and I shall be alone gazing at the autumn moon."

He was deeply interested, and being uncertain in thought said : " Even the poets of the Tang Empire[1] could not decide which to praise most, Spring or Autumn. Your decisions make me think that there must be some personal reasons when our inclination is touched or charmed. Our souls are imbued with the colours of the sky, moon, or flowers of that moment. I desire much to know how you came to know the charms of Spring and Autumn. The moon of a winter night is given as an instance of dreariness, and as it is very cold I had never seen it intentionally. When I went down to Isé to be present as the messenger of the King at the ceremony[2] of installing the virgin in charge of the shrine, I wanted to come back in the early dawn, so went to take leave of the Princess [whose installation had just taken

[1] Famous period in Chinese history.
[2] This gentleman's name is known.

place] in a moon-bright night after many days' snow, half shrinking to think of my journey.

" Her residence was an other-worldly place awful even to the imagination, but she called me into an adequate apartment. There were persons [in that room] who had come down in the reign of the Emperor Enyu.[1] Their aspect was very holy, ancient, and mystical. They told of the things of long ago with tears. They brought out a well-tuned four-stringed lute. The music did not seem to be anything happening in this world ; I regretted that day should even dawn, and was touched so deeply that I had almost forgotten about returning to the Capital. Ever since then the snowy nights of winter recall that scene, and I without fail gaze at the moon even though hugging the fire. You will surely understand me, and hereafter every dark night with gentle rain will touch my heart ; I feel this has not been inferior to the snowy night at the palace of the Isé virgin."

With these words he departed and I thought he could not have known who I was.

In the Eighth month of the next year [1043] we went again to the Imperial Palace, and there was in the Court an entertainment throughout the night. I did not know that he was present at it, and I passed that night in my own room. When I looked out [in early morning] opening the sliding doors on the corridor I saw the morning moon very faint and beautiful. I heard footsteps and people approached—some reciting sutras. One of them came to the entrance, and

[1] He ruled from 970 to 984. It was now 1042.

51

addressed me. I replied, and he, suddenly remembering, exclaimed, " That night of softly falling rain I do not forget, even for a moment ! I yearn for it." As chance did not permit me many words I said :

> *What intensity of memory clings to your heart?*
> *That gentle shower fell on the leaves—*
> *Only for a moment [our hearts touched].*

I had scarcely said so when people came up and I stole back without his answer.

That evening, after I had gone to my room, my companion came in to tell me that he had replied to my poem : " If there be such a tranquil night as that of the rain, I should like in some way to make you listen to my lute, playing all the songs I can remember."

I wanted to hear it, and waited for the fit occasion, but there was none, ever.

In the next year one tranquil evening I heard that he had come into the Princess's Palace, so I crept out of my chamber with my companion, but there were many people waiting within and without the Palace, and I turned back. He must have been of the same mind with me. He had come because it was so still a night, and he returned because it was noisy.

> *I yearn for a tranquil moment*
> *To be out upon the sea of harmony,*
> *In that enchanted boat.*
> *Oh, boatman, do you know my heart?*

So I composed that poem — and there is nothing more to tell. His personality was very excellent and he was not an ordinary man, but time passed, and neither called to the other.

In Winter, though the snow had not come yet, the starlit sky was clear and cold. One whole night I talked with those who were in the Palace . . . [1]

Like a good-for-nothing woman I retired from the Court life.

On the twenty-fifth of the End month [Christmas Day, 1043] I was summoned by the Princess to the religious service of reciting Buddha's names. I went for that night only. About forty ladies were there all dressed in deep-red dresses and also in deep-red outer robe. I sat behind the person who led me in—the most shadow-like person among them—and I retired before dawn. On my way home it snowed in fluttering flakes, and the frozen, ghostly moon was reflected in my dull-red sleeves of glossy silk. Even that reflection seemed to be wet and sad. I thought all the way : " The year comes to a close and the night also—and the moon reflected in my sleeve—all passes. When one is in Court, one may become familiar with those who serve there, and know worldly things better, and if one is thought amiable one is received as a lady and favours may be bestowed "—such had been my thought, but father was now disappointed in me and kept me at home ; but how could I expect that my fortunes should become dazzling in

[1] Something seems to have occurred which may have been her marriage to a noble of lower rank or inferior family than her own, but one can only infer this, she does not tell it.

53

a moment? It was father's idle fancy, yet he felt that it had betrayed him.

Though a thousand times, how many! I gathered parsley[1]
  in the fields
    Yet my wishes were by no means fulfilled.

I grumbled so far, and no farther.

I regretted deeply the idle fancies of old days, and as my parents would not accompany me to temples [on pilgrimages] I could hardly suppress my impatience. I wish to strengthen my spirit to bring up my child who is still in the germ. Moreover, I wish to do my best to pile up virtuous deeds for the life to come, so encouraging my heart I went to the Ishiyama Temple after the twentieth day of the Frost month [1045]. It snowed and the route was lovely. On coming in sight of the barrier at Osaka Pass, I was reminded that it was also in Winter when I passed it on my way up to Kyoto. Then also it was a windy tempestuous day.

The sound of the Autumn wind at the barrier of Osaka!
  It differs not from that heard long ago.

The temple at Seki, magnificent though it was, made me think of the old roughly hewn Buddha. The beach at Uchidé has not changed in the passing of months and years, but my own heart feels change.

Towards evening I arrived at the temple and after

---

[1] There is an old fable about parsley: A country person ate parsley and thought it very fine, so he went up to the Capital to present it to the King, but the King was not so much pleased, for he could not find it good. So " to gather parsley " means to endeavour to win others' favour by offering something we care for but others do not.

a bath went up to the main shrine. The mountain wind was dreadful. I took it for a good omen that, falling asleep in the temple [I heard a voice], saying : " From the inner shrine perfume has been bestowed. Tell it at once." At the words I awoke, and passed the night in prayer.

The next day the wind raged and it snowed heavily.

I comforted my lonely heart with the friend of the Princess who came with me. We left after three days.

On the twenty-fifth of the Tenth month of the next year [1046] the Capital was in great excitement over the purification ceremonies before the Great Ceremony.[1]

For my part I wanted to set out that same day for Hasé [Temple] for my own religious purification. They stopped me, saying it was a sight to be seen only once in one reign ; that even the country-people come to see the procession, and it was madness to leave the city that very day. " Your deeds will be spread abroad and people will gossip about you," said my brother angrily. " No, no, let the person have her own will " ; and according to my wish he [her husband] let me start. His kindness touched me, but on the other hand I pitied those who accompanied me [her retinue], who with longing hearts wanted to see the ceremony.

But what have we to do with such shows ? Buddha will be pleased with those who come at a time like this. I wanted without fail to receive the divine favour, and started before dawn. When I was cross-

[1] The enthronement ceremony of Emperor Goreizei, from 1046 to 1068.

ing the great bridge of Nijo, with pine torches flaming before me, and with my attendants in pure white robes, all the men on horseback, in carriage, or on foot who encountered me on their way to the stands prepared for sight-seers said, in surprise, " What is that ?" and some even laughed or scolded me. As I was passing before the gate of Yoshinori the Commander of the Bodyguard and his men were standing there before the wide-open portals. They said, laughing, 'Here goes a company to the temple—there are many days and months in the world [to do that in]!" But there was one [standing by] who said : " What is it to fatten the eyes for a moment ? They are firmly determined. They will surely receive Buddha's favour; we ought also to make up our minds [for the good] without sight-seeing." Thus one man spoke seriously.

I had wanted to leave the city before broad daylight, and had started in the middle of the night, but had to wait for belated persons till the very thick fog became thinner. People flowed in from the country like a river. Nobody could turn aside to make room for anybody else, and even the ill-behaved and vulgar children, who passed beside my carriage with some difficulty, had words of wonder and contempt for us.

I felt sorry that I had started that day, yet praying to Buddha with all my heart, I arrived at the ferry of Uji. Even there the people were coming up to the city in throngs, and the ferry-man, seeing these numberless people, was filled with his own importance, and grew proud. He, tucking up his sleeves against his face and leaning on his pole, would not bring the boat at once. He looked around whistling and assumed an indifferent air. We could not cross the river for a long time, so I looked around the place, which I had felt a curiosity to see, ever since reading Genji-monogatari which tells that the daughter of the Princess of Uji lived here. I thought it a charming spot. At last we managed to get across the river and went to see the Uji mansion.[1] I was at once reminded that the Lady Ukifuné [of the romance] had been living here.

As we had started before daybreak, my people were tired out, and rested at Hiroichi to take food. The guard said: " Is that the famous mountain Kurikoma? It is towards evening, be ready with your armour" [to protect from robbers or evil spirits]. I listened to these words with a shudder, but we passed that mountain [without adventure] and the sun was on its summit when we arrived at the lake of Nieno. They went in several directions to seek a lodging and returned saying there was no proper place, only an obscure hut ; but as there was no other place we took that.

In the house there were only two men, for the rest had all gone to the Capital. Those two men did not sleep that night at all, but kept watch around the

[1] This is called the Byōdōin and is one of the famous buildings now existing in Japan (see illustrations in Cram's *Impressions of Japanese Architecture*), built upon an exquisite design, and original in character. It had been the villa of the Prime Minister, but was made into a temple in 1051, when the riches of the interior decorations were more like the gorgeousness of Indian temples than the chaster decorations of Japan.

house. My maids who were in the recess [perhaps the outer part of the hut used as kitchen] asked, "Why do you walk about so?" and the men answered, "Why? we have rented our house to perfect strangers. What should we do if our kettles were stolen? Of course we cannot sleep!" I felt both dread and laughter to hear them.

In the early morning we left there and knelt before the great East Temple.[1] The temple at Iso-no-Kami was antique and on the verge of ruin. That night we lodged at the Yamabé Temple. Although I was tired out, I recited sutras and went to sleep. In my dream I saw a very noble and pure woman. At her coming the wind blew deliciously. She found me out, and said, smiling, " For what purpose have you come?" I answered, " How could I help coming?" [since you are here], and she said, " You would better be in the Imperial Court, and become intimate with the Lady Hakasé." I was very much delighted and encouraged.

We crossed the river and arrived at the Hatsusé Temple at night. After purifying, I went up to the Temple. I remained three days, and slept expecting to start in the morning. At midnight I dreamt that a cedar twig[2] was thrown into the room as a token bestowed by the Inari god. I was startled, but waking found it only a dream.

[1] At Nara where the great Buddha, 160 feet high, was already standing.
[2] In those days it was the custom for the person who wished to be favoured by the Inari god to crown his head with a twig of cedar. The Inari god was then the god of the rice-plant. He is now confused with the fox-god whose little shrines, flanked by small stone foxes, are seen everywhere.

We began our return journey after midnight, and as we could not find a lodging, we again passed a night in a very small house, which seemed to be a very curious one somehow. " Do not sleep ! Something unexpected will happen !" " Dont't be frightened !" " Lie down even without breathing !" This was said and I spent the night in loneliness and dread. I felt that I lived a thousand years that night, and when the day dawned I saw that we were in a robbers' den. People said that the mistress of that house lived by a strange occupation.

We crossed the Uji River in a high wind and the ferry-boat passed very near the fishing seine.

Years have passed and only sounds of waters have come to my ears,
To-day, indeed, I may even count the ripples around the fishing net.

[This poem may seem a little obscure. It means that her own life had been lived long in a kind of dreamland of her own creating, but was gradually emerging into reality.]

If, as I am doing now, I continue to write down events four or five years after they have happened, my life will seem to be that of a pilgrim, but it is not so. I am jotting down the happenings of several years. In the spring I went to the Kurama Temple. It was a soft spring day, with mist trailing over the mountain-side. The mountain people brought tokoro [a kind of root] as the only food and I found it good. When I left there flowers were already gone.

In Gods-absent month I went again, and the mountain views along the way were more beautiful than before, the mountain-side brocaded with the autumn colours. The stream, rushing headlong, boiled up like molten metal and then shattered into crystals.

When I reached the monastery the maple leaves, wet with a shower, were brilliant beyond compare.

The pattern of the maple leaves in Autumn dyed with the rain—
Beautiful in the deep mountain!

After two years or so I went again to Ishiyama. It semeed to be raining, and I heard some one saying rain is disagreeable on a journey, but on opening the door I found the waning moon lighting even the depths of the ravine. What I thought rain was the stream rippilng below the roots of the trees.

The sound of the mountain brook gives an illusion of rain drops,
Yet the calm of the waning moon shines over all.

The next time I went to Hasé Temple, my journey was not so solitary as before. Along the route various persons invited me to ceremonious dinners, and we made but slow progress. The autumn woods were beautiful at the Hahasono forest in Yamashiro. I crossed the Hasé River. We stayed there for three days. This time we were too many to lodge in that small house on the other side of the Nara Pass, so we camped in the field. Our men passed the night lying on mukabaki[1] spread on the grass. They could not

[1] A kind of leathern shield made of untanned deerskin worn hanging from the shoulder.

sleep for the dew which fell on their heads. The moon clear and more picturesque than elsewhere.

> *Even in our wandering journey,*
> *The lonely moon accompanies us lighting us from the sky,*
> *The waning moon I used to gaze at in the Royal City.*

As I could do as I liked, I went even to distant temples for worship, and my heart was consoled through both the pleasures and fatigues of the way. Though it was half diversion, yet it (her prayers) gave me hope. I had no pressing sorrow in those days and tried to bring up my boy in the manner I thought best, and was impatient of passing time. The man I depended upon (her husband) wished to attain to happiness like other people, and the future looked promising. A dear friend of mine, who used to exchange poems with me and continued to write, through many changes of situation, although not so often as of old, married the Governor of Echizen and went down to that Province. After that all communication between us ceased, so I wrote her a poem finding the means of sending it with great difficulty :

> *Undying affection !*
> *Can it end at last, overlaid with time*
> *Even as snow covers the land in the Northern Province ?*

She wrote back :

> *Even a little pebble does not cease to be,*
> *Though pressed under the snow of Hakusan ;*
> *So is my affection even though hidden.*

I went down to a hollow of Nishiyama (in the western hills of Kyoto). There were flowers blooming in confusion. It was beautiful, yet lonely. There was no sight of man. A tranquil haze enclosed us.

> *Far from towns, in the heart of the mountain,*
> *The cherry blooms, and wastes its blooms away*
> *With none to see.*

When the sorrow of the World[1] troubled my heart I made a retreat in the Uzumasa Temple. To me there arrived a letter from one who served the Princess. While I was answering it the temple bell was heard.

> *The outer world of many sorrows*
> *Is not to be forgotten even here.*
> *At the sound of the evening bell*
> *Lonely grows my heart.*

To the beautifully tranquil palace of the Princess I went one day to talk with two congenial friends. The next day, finding life rather tedious, I thought longingly of them and sent a poem :[2]
One wrote back :
And the other :

> *Knowing the place of our meeting to be the sea of tears,*
> *Where memories ripple, and affections flow back,*
> *Yet we ventured into it—and my longing for you grew stronger*
> *than ever.*
> *We ventured into that sea,*
> *To find the pearls of consolement,*
> *No pearls, but drops of sad, sweet tears we found!*

[1] The World : i.e. her husband.
[2] The following poems have been found impossible of literal translation on account of play of words.

Of Old Japan

Who would venture into the sea of tears
Seeking for the chance with zealous care,
Had not the flowers of lovely vision floated in it !
Tell her, oh, western-going moon,
That dreaming of her I could sleep no more,
But all the night
My pillow was bedewed with loving tears.

That friend being of the same mind with me, we used to talk over every joy and sorrow of the world, but she went down to the Province of Chikuzen in Kyushu (extreme southwest of old Japan). On a moon-bright night I went to bed thinking of her with longing, for in the palace we had been wont not to sleep on such a night, but to sit up gazing into the sky. I dreamed that we were in the palace and saw each other as we had done in reality. I awoke startled; the moon was then near the western ridge of the mountain and I thought " I would I had not wakened "[1] (quoting from a famous poem).

In the Autumn (1056) I had occasion to go down to the Province of Izumi.[2] To do the journey was very picturesque. We passed a night at Takahama. It was dark, and in the depths of the night I heard the sound of an oar, and was told that a singer had come. My companions called her boat to come alongside ours. She was lighted by a distant fire, her sleeves

---

[1] *As I slept fondly thinking of him*
He appeared to my sight—
Oh, I would I had not wakened
To find it only a dream !
[2] Her brother Sadayoshi was Governor of that Province.

were long, she shaded her face with a fan and sung.
She was charming. The next evening, when the sun
was still on the mountain-top, we passed the beach of
Sumiyoshi. It was seen all in mist, and pine branches,
the surface of the sea, and the beach where waves
rolled up, combined to make a scene more beautiful
than a picture.

> *It is an evening of Autumn*
> *—The seashore of Sumiyoshi !*
> *Can words describe it ?*
> *What can be compared with it ?*

Even after the boat was towed along, I looked back
again and again, never satiated.

In the winter I returned to Kyoto. We took our
boat at Oé Bay. That night a tempest raged with
such fury that the very rocks seemed to be shaken.
The god of Thunder[1] came roaring, and the sound of
dashing waves, the tumult of the wind, the horrors of
the sea, made me feel that life was coming to an end.
But they dragged the boat ashore, where we spent the
night. The rain stopped, but not the wind, and we
could not start. We passed five or six days on these
wide-stretching sands. When the wind had gone
down a little, I looked out, rolling up the curtain of
my cabin. The evening tide was rising swiftly and
cranes called to each other in the bay.

People of the Province came in crowds to see us,
and said that if the boat had been outside the bay that
night it would have been seen no more. Even the
thought terrified me.

64

Of Old Japan

Off Ishitsu, in the wild sea
The boat driven before the storm
Fades away and is seen no more.

The wild gusts drive the boat—
Into the wild sea she disappears—
Off Ishitsu !

I devoted myself in various ways for the World [her husband]. Even in serving at Court one had likewise to devote one's self unceasingly. What favor could one win by returning to the parents' home from time to time ?

As I advanced in age I felt it unbecoming to behave as young couples do. While I was lamenting I grew ill, and could not go out to temples for worship. Even this rare going out was stopped, and I had no hope of living long, but I wanted to give my young children a safer position while I was alive.

I grieved and waited for the delightful thing [an appointment] for my husband. In Autumn he got a position,[1] but not so good a one as we had hoped, and we were much disappointed. It was not so distant as the place from which he had returned, so he made up his mind to go, and we hastily made preparations. He started from the house where his daughter had recently gone to live.[2] It was after the tenth of the Gods-absent month. I could not know what had

[1] In 1017, as Governor of Shinano Province.
[2] She was thirty-five years old and her husband forty-one years old when they were married. We may suppose that she was his second wife. This daughter must have been borne by the first wife. The cause of starting from his daughter's house is some superstitious idea, and not the coldness of their relation.

happened after he started, but all seemed happy on that day. He was accompanied by our boy. My husband wore a red coat and pale purple kimono'[1] and aster-coloured hakama [divided skirt], and carried a long sword. The boy wore blue figured clothes and red hakama, and they mounted their horses beside the veranda.

When they had gone out noisily I felt very, very lonely. As I had heard the Province was not so distant I was less hopeless than I had been before.

The people who accompanied him to see him off returned the next day and told me that they had gone down with great show [of splendour] and, then continuing, said they had seen human fire[2] this morning starting [form the company] and flying towards the Capital. I tried to suppose it to be from some one of his retinue. How could I think the worst? I could think of nothing but how to bring up these younger ones.

He came back in the Deutzia month of the next year and passed the Summer and Autumn at home, and on the twenty-fifth of the Long-night month he became ill.

1058. On the fifth day of the Tenth month all became like a dream.[3] My sorrows could be compared to nothing in this world.

[1] The rank of the person determined the colour of his clothes. Red was worn by nobles of the fifth degree.

[2] The Japanese believed that " human fire " or spirit can be seen leaving the body of one who is soon to die.

[3] Her husband died.

Now I knew that my present state had been reflected in the mirror offered to the Hasé Temple [about twenty-five years before by her mother] where some one was seen weeping in agony. The reflection of the happier one had not been realized. That could never be in the future.

On the twenty-third we burnt his remains with despairing hearts, my boy, who went down with him last Autumn, being dressed exquisitely and much attended, followed the bier weeping in black clothes with hateful things [mourning insignia] on them. My feeling when I saw him going out can never be expressed. I seemed to wander in dreams and thought that human life must soon cease here. If I had not given myself up to idle fictions [she herself had written several] and poetry, but had practised religious austerities night and day, I would not have seen such a dream-world.

At Hasé Temple a cedar branch was cast down to me by the Inari god and this thing [the loss of her husband] would not have happened if I had visited the Inari shrine on my way home. The dreams which I had seen in these past years which bid me pray to the Heaven Illuminating Honoured Goddess meant that I should have been in the Imperial Court as a nurse, sheltered behind the favour of the King and Queen—so the dream interpreter interpreted my dream, but I could not realize this. Only the sorrowful reflection in the mirror was realized unaltered. O pitiful and sorrowful I ! Thus nothing could happen as I willed, and I wandered in this world doing no virtuous deed for the future life.

Life seemed to survive sorrows, but I was uneasy at the thought that things would happen against my will, even in the future life. There was only one thing I could rely on.

Ceaseless tears—clouded mind:
Bright scene—moon-shadow.

On the thirteenth of the Tenth month [1055] I dreamed one night this dream :

There in the garden of my house at the farthest ledge stood Amitabha Buddha ! He was not seen distinctily, but as if through a cloud. I could snatch a glimpse now and then when the cloud lifted. The lotus-flower pedestal was three or four feet above the ground ; the Buddha was about six feet high.

Golden light shone forth ; one hand was extended, the fingers of the other were bent in form of benediction. None but I could see him, yet I felt such reverence that I dared not approach the blind to see him better. None but I might hear him saying, " Then this time I will go back, and afterwards come again to receive you." I was startled and awoke into the fourteenth day. *This dream only was my hope for the life to come.*[1]

I had lived with my husband's nephews, but after that sad event we parted not to meet again. One very dark night I was visited by the nephew who was

[1] At death the Lord Buddha coming on a cloud appears to the faithful one and accompanies the soul to Heaven.

living at Rokuhara ; I could not but welcome so
rare a guest.

> *No moon, and darkness deepens*
> *Around Obasuté. Why have you come ?*
> *It cannot be to see the moon !*[1]

After that time [the death of her husband] an intimate friend stopped all communication.

> *She may be thinking that I*
> *Am no more in this world, yet my days*
> *Are wasted in weeping.*

In the Tenth month I turned, my eyes full of tears,
towards the intensely bright moon.

> *Even into the mind always clouded with grief,*
> *There is cast the reflection of the bright moon.*

Years and months passed away. Whenever I
recollected the dream-like incident [of his death] my
mind was troubled and my eyes filled so that I cannot think distinctly of those days.

My people went to live elsewhere and I remained
alone in my solitary home. I was tired of meditation
and sent a poem to one who had not called on me for
a long time.

> *Weeds grow before my gate*
> *And my sleeves are wet with dew,*
> *No one calls on me,*

[1] The point of this is in the name of the place, Obasuté, which may be
translated, " Aunt Casting Away." It is a place famous for the beauty
of its scenery in moonlight.

Diaries of Court Ladies

My tears are solitary—alas!

She was a nun and she sent an answer :

The weeds before a dwelling house
May remind you of me!
Bushes bury the hut
Where lives the world-deserted one.

II

THE DIARY OF MURASAKI SHIKIBU

II

THE DIARY OF MURASAKI SHIKIBU[1]

A.D. 1007—1010

As the autumn season approaches the Tsuchimikado[2] becomes inexpressibly smile-giving. The tree-tops near the pond, the bushes near the stream, are dyed in varying tints whose colours grow deeper in the mellow light of evening. The murmuring sound of waters mingles all the night through with the never-ceasing recitation[3] of sutras which appeal more to one's heart as the breezes grow cooler.

The ladies waiting upon her honoured presence are talking idly. The Queen hears them ; she must find them annoying, but she conceals it calmly. Her beauty needs no words of mine to praise it, but I cannot help feeling that to be near so beautiful a queen will be the only relief from my sorrow. So in spite of my better desires [for a religious life] I am here. Nothing else dispels my grief[4]—it is wonderful !

It is still the dead of night, the moon is dim and darkness lies under the trees. We hear an officer call, " The outer doors of the Queen's apartment must be

[1] This diary seems to have been jotted down in disconnected paragraphs and the editors have preserved that form.

[2] Tsuchimikado : the residence of Prime Minister Fujiwara, the father of the Queen.

[3] Priests are praying for the easy delivery of the Queen, who has gone to her parents' house before the birth, in accordance with old Japanese custom.

[4] The writer of this diary lost her husband in 1001.

73

opened. The maids-of-honour are not yet come—
let the Queen's secretaries come forward!" While
this order is being given the three-o'clock bell re-
sounds, startling the air. Immediately the prayers at
the five altars[1] begin. The voices of the priests in
loud recitation, vying with each other far and near,
are solemn indeed. The Abbot of the Kanon-in
Temple, accompanied by twenty priests, comes from
the eastern[2] side building to pray. Even their footsteps along the gallery which sound to'-do-ro to'-do-ro
are sacred. The head priest of the Hoju Temple goes
to the mansion near the race-track, the prior of the
Henji Temple goes to the library. I follow with my
eyes when the holy figures in pure white robes cross
the stately Chinese bridge and walk along the broad
path. Even Azaliah Saisa bends the body in reverence before the deity Daiitoku. The maids-of-
honour arrive at dawn.

I can see the garden from my room beside the entrance to the gallery. The air is misty, the dew is still
on the leaves. The Lord Prime Minister is walking
there ; he orders his men to cleanse the brook. He
breaks off a stalk of ominaeshi [flower maiden] which
is in full bloom by the south end of the bridge. He
peeps in over my screen ! His noble appearance em-
barrasses us, and I am ashamed of my morning [not
yet painted and powdered] face. He says, "Your
poem on this ! If you delay so much the fun is gone !"

[1] Altars before Fudō, Gosansé, Gunsari, Daiitoku, Kongōyasha.
[2] See the plan of a great house of those days.

OLD PRINT OF A NOBLEMAN'S DWELLING IN
THE AZUMAYA STYLE

The Tsuchimikado, or Prime Minister's mansion, must have been like this.

and I seized the chance to run away to the writing-box, hiding my face—

> *Flower-maiden in bloom—*
> *Even more beautiful for the bright dew,*
> *Which is partial, and never favours me.*

"So prompt!" said he, smiling, and ordered a writing-box to be brought [for himself].

His answer :

> *The silver dew is never partial.*
> *From her heart*
> *The flower-maiden's beauty.*

One wet and calm evening I was talking with Lady Saishō. The young Lord[1] of the Third Rank sat with the misu[2] partly rolled up. He seemed maturer than his age and was very graceful. Even in light conversation such expressions as "Fair soul is rarer than fair face" come gently to his lips, covering us with confusion. It is a mistake to treat him like a young boy. He keeps his dignity among ladies, and I saw in him a much-sought-after romantic hero when once he walked off reciting to himself :

> *Linger in the field where flower-maidens are blooming*
> *And your name will be tarnished with tales of gallantry.*

Some such trifle as that sometimes lingers in my mind when really interesting things are soon forgotten—why ?

[1] Yorimichi, the Prime Minister Fujiwara Michinaga's son, who was then sixteen years old.

[2] Misu : a thin finely woven bamboo curtain, behind which one may see but not be seen, hung before great personages and women's apartments.

Nowadays people are carrying pretty folding fans.

Since the twentieth of the Eighth month, the more favoured court nobles and officers have been on night duty, passing the nights in the corridor, or on the mats of the veranda idly amusing themselves. Young men who are unskilled in koto or fué [harp or flute] amuse themselves with tonearasoi[1] and imayō,[2] and at such a time this is entertaining. Narinobu, the Queen's Grand Chamberlain, Tsunefusa, the Lieutenant-General of the Left Bodyguard and State Councillor, and Narimasa, the Major-General of the Bodyguard and Governor of Mino, passed the night in diversions. The Lord Prime Minister must have been apprehensive, for he has forbidden all public entertainment. Those who have long retired from the court have come in crowds to ask after the Queen's welfare, so we have had no peace.

Twenty-sixth day. We finished the preparation of perfume[3] and distributed it to all. A number of us who had been making it into balls assembled together. On my way from Her Majesty's chamber I peeped into Ben Saishō's room. She was sleeping. She wore garments of hagi[4] and shion[4] over which she had put a strongly perfumed lustrous robe. Her face was

---

[1] Tonearasoi : at present not known.

[2] Imayō, or " new style," a kind of song in vogue in those days. The verse consists of eight or ten alternating seven- and five-syllable lines.

[3] This perfume was composed of purified Borneo camphor, aloe wood and musk, and was used to perfume clothing, etc.

[4] Hagi : violet-coloured dress with blue lining, the violet dye taken from sapan-wood ; Shion : pale purple dress with blue lining.

hidden behind the cloth ;[1] her head rested on a writing-case of gold lacquer. Her forehead was beautiful and fascinating. She seemed like a princess in a picture. I took off the cloth which hid her mouth and said, "You are just like the heroine of a romance!" She blushed, half rising ; she was beauty itself. She is always beautiful, but on this occasion her charm was wonderfully heightened.

Dear Lady Hyoé brought me some floss[2] silk for chrysanthemums. "The wife of the Prime Minister favours you with this present to drive away age,[2] carefully use it and then throw it away."

May that lady live one thousand years who guards the flowers!
My sleeves are wet with thankful tears
As though I had been walking
In a garden of dewy chrysanthemums.

I wanted to send it, but as I heard that she had gone away I kept it.

The evening I went to the Queen's chamber. As the moon was beautiful, skirts overflowed from beneath the misu.[3] By and by there came Lady Koshōshō and Lady Dainagon. Her Majesty took out some of the perfume which had been made the other day and put it into an incense burner to try it. The

---

[1] A face covering used while sleeping.

[2] Floss silk was used to protect chrysanthemum flowers from frost. The flower itself was believed to have the virtue of lengthening life. The Imperial garden party undoubtedly originated from a belief in this virtue in the flower.

[3] Ladies were crowded close behind the misu looking at the moon,

77

garden was admirable—" When the ivy leaves become red !" they were saying—but our Lady seemed less tranquil than usual. The priests came for prayers, and I went into the inside room but was called away and finally went to my own chamber. I wanted only to rest a few minutes, but fell asleep. By midnight everybody was in great excitement.

Tenth day of the Long-moon month.

When day began to dawn the decorations[1] of the Queen's chamber were changed and she removed to a white bed. The Prime Minister, his sons, and other noblemen made haste to change the curtains or the screens, the bed cover, and other things.[1] All day long she lay ill at ease. Men cried at the top of their voices to scare away evil spirits. There assembled not only the priests who had been summoned here for these months, but also itinerant monks who were brought from every mountain and temple. Their prayers would reach to the Buddhas of the three worlds. All the soothsayers in the world were summoned. Eight million gods seemed to be listening with ears erect for their Shinto prayers. Messengers ran off to order sutra-reciting at various temples ; thus the night was passed. On the east side of the screen [placed around the Queen's bed] there assembled the ladies of the Court. On the west side there were lying the Queen's substitutes possessed with [or who were enticing] the evil spirits.[2]

[1] Hangings, screens, and clothes of attendants were all white at the time of a birth.

[2] Which would otherwise have attacked the Queen. Some of the ladies-

Each was lying surrounded by a pair of folding screens. The joints of the screens were curtained and priests were appointed to cry sutras there. On the south side there sat in many rows abbots and other dignitaries of the priesthood, who prayed and swore till their voices grew hoarse, as if they were bringing down the living form of Fudō.[1] The space between the north room and the dais [on which was the Queen's bed] was very narrow, yet when I thought of it afterwards I counted more than forty persons who were standing there. They could not move at all, and grew so dizzy that they could remember nothing. The people [i.e. the ladies-in-waiting and maids-of-honour] now coming from home could not enter the main apartment at all. There was no place for their flowing robes and long sleeves. Certain older women wept secretly.

Eleventh day. At dawn the north sliding doors were taken away to throw the two rooms together. The Queen was moved towards the veranda. As there was no time to hang misu, she was surrounded by kichō. The Reverend Gyochō and the other priests performed incantations. The Reverend Ingen recited the prayer written by the Lord Prime Minister on the previous day adding some grave vows

in-waiting undertook this duty There is a difference of opinion between the translators as to whehter this was done with the intention of deceiving the evil spirits into attacking the wrong person (by introducing into her neighbourhood other women surrounded with screens and attendants) or by transmitting the supposed evil spirits out of the Queen into her ladies by a sort of mesmerization.

[1] Fudo : a terrible-looking Buddhist idol who was thought to have the power to subdue all evil spirits.

of his own. His words were infinitely august and hopeful. The Prime Minister joining in the prayer, we felt more assured of a fortunate delivery. Yet there was still lingering anxiety which made us very sad, and many eyes were filled with tears. We said, "Tears are not suitable to this occasion," but we could not help crying. They said that Her Majesty suffered more because the rooms were too crowded, so the people were ordered to the south and east rooms. After this there remained in the Royal Apartment only the more important personages. The Prime Minister, Lady Sanuki, and Lady Saishō were within the [Royal] screen. The honoured priest of Ninna Temple and the court priest of Mii Temple were summoned within. The Prime Minister gave various commands, and his voice overpowered those of the priests. There were also Ladies Dainagon, Koshōshō, Miya-no-Naishi, Nakatsukasa-no-Kimi, Taifu-no-Myobu, Daishikibu-no-Omoto, Tono-no-Senji—these last were venerable ladies of experience, but even they were bewildered with good reason. I am yet a novice, and I felt with all my heart that the occasion was serious. Also, in the place a little behind, outside the curtain, there were the nurses of the Princesses Naishi-no-Kami and Nakatsukasa, of the Queen's sister Shōnagon, and of her younger sister Koshikibu. These nurses forced their way into the narrow passage behind the two screens and there walked back and forth, so that none could pass that way. There were many other persons bustling about, but I could not distinguish them. The Prime Minis-

ter's son, Lieutenant-General Saisho, Major-General
Masamichi of the Fourth Rank, not to speak of
Lieutenant-General Tsunefusa, of the Left Bodyguard, and Miya-no-Taifu, who had not known Her
Majesty familiarly, all looked over her screen for some
time. They showed eyes swollen up with weeping
[over her sufferings], forgetting the shame of it. On
their heads rice[1] was scattered white as snow. Their
rumpled clothes must have been unseemly, but we
could only think of those things afterward. A part
of the Queen's head was shaved.[2] I was greatly
astonished and very sorry to see it, but she was
delivered peacefully. The after-birth was delayed,
and all priests crowded to the south balcony, under
the eaves of the magnificent main building, while
those on the bridge recited sutras more passionately,
often kneeling.

Among the ladies-in-waiting on the east side were
seen some of the courtiers.[3] Lady Kochujō's eye met
that of the Lieutenant-General. People afterwards
laughed over her astonished expression. She is a
very fascinating and elegant person, nad is always
very careful to adorn her face. This morning she
had done so, but her eyes were red, and her rouge was
spoiled by tears. She was disfigured, and hardly

[1] For good luck.
[2] So that she might be ordained as a priestess and insured a good recep-
tion in the next world, only done when the sick person is in great danger.
[3] This was contrary to etiquette and shows the extreme excitement of
the moment. Ladies and gentlemen of the court remained in separate
rooms on social occasions.

seemed the same person. The imperfectly made-up
face of Lady Saishō was a rare sight, but what about
my own? It is lucky for me that people cannot
notice such things at such a time.

As the after-birth came, it was fearful to hear the
jealously swearing voices of the evil spirits. Shinyo-
Azari took charge of Lady Gen-no-Kurōdo; Sōso
took charge of Hyoé-no-Kurōdo; a priest Hojuji
took charge of Ukon-no-Kurōdo;[1] Chisō Azari
took charge of Lady Miya-no-Naishi. This last
priest was overpowered with the evil spirit, and as he
was in a too pitiable state Nenkaku Azari went to help
him. It was not because his prayer had little virtue, but the [evil] spirit was too strong. Priest Eikō
was in charge of Lady Saishō's supplicator of the
spirit [i.e. Queen's substitute]. This priest swore all
night till his voice became hoarse. Most ladies who
were summoned in order that the spirits might enter
into them remained safe, and they were much troubled [thinking that it would be to the Queen's advantage were they attacked]. At noon we felt that the
sun came out at last. The Queen was at ease!

She is now at peace. Incomparable joy! Moreover, it is a prince, so the joy cannot be oblique. The
court ladies who had passed the previous day in
anxiety, not knowing what to do, as if they were lost
in the mist of the early morning, went one by one to
rest in their own rooms, so that before the Queen
there remained only some elderly persons proper for

[1] Kurodo = secretary (in charge of court manuscripts.)

82

such occasions. The Lord Prime Minister and his Lady went away to give offerings to the priest who had read sutras and performed religious austerities during the past months, and to those doctors who were recently summoned. The doctors and sooth-sayers, who had invented special forms of efficacy, were given pensions. Within the house they were perhaps preparing for the ceremony of bathing the child.

Large packages [of ceremonial clothes[1]] were carried to the apartments of the ladies-in-waiting. Karaginu[2] and embroidered[2] trains were worn. Some wore dazzlingly brilliant trains embroidered and ornamented with mother-of-pearl. Some lamented that the fans which had been ordered had not come. They all painted and powdered. When I looked from the bridge I saw Her Majesty's first officials, and the highest officers of His Highness the Crown Prince [the newborn child] and other court nobles. The Prime Minister went out to have the brook, which had been choked with mud, cleaned[3] out.

All the people seem happy. Even those who have some cause for melancholy are overtaken by the general joy. The First Official of our Queen has naturally seemed happier than anybody, though he does not show special smiles of self-satisfaction and pride.

[1] Everybody was still wearing white, colour of purification.
[2] See frontispiece.
[3] Every Japanese family does this to-day, for almost all gardens have artificial brooks or ponds.

The Lieutenant-General of the Light Bodyguard has been joking with the King's Adviser of the Middle Rank, sitting on a mat on the balcony of the side building. The sword of His Highness the young Prince has been brought from the Imperial Court. The Lieutenant-General, and First Secretary Yorisada, on his way home from the shrine at Ise[1] where he had gone as Imperial Messenger to offer nusa,[2] stopped at the gate [as he could not enter the house[3]] to inquire for Her Majesty. He was given some present, I did not see it.

The navel cord was cut by the Prime Minister's Lady. Lady Tachibana of the Third Rank gave the breast for the first time [ceremonial]. For the wet-nurse Daisaémon-no-Omoto was chosen, for she has been in the Court a long time and is very familiar with it ; the daughter of Munetoki, courtier and Governor of Bitchū, and the nurse of Kurodo-no-Ben were also chosen as nurses.

The ceremony of bathing was performed at six o'clock in the evening. The bath was lighted [by torches]. The Queen's maid in white over green

[1] Imperial shrine at Isé : the oldest shrine, built 3 B.C., dedicated to the Heaven Shining Goddess, ancestor of the Imperial family. This shrine is rebuilt every twenty years on the same model. It is the most sacred spot in Japan, and all serious events pertaining to the Empire or Imperial Household are announced there to the Goddess-Ancestor by Imperial Messenger.

[2] Nusa : rolls of silk or paper offered by a worshipper.

[3] Because a birth in a house was defilement, while a messenger to or from a god was holy.

84

prepared the hot water. The stand for the bath-tub was covered with white cloth.

Chikamitsu, Governor of Owari [Province], and Nakanobu, the Head Officer attached to the Queen, presented themselves before the misu.

There were two stands for kettles.

Lady Kyoiko and Lady Harima poured the cold water. Two ladies, Ōmoku and Uma, selected six-teen jars from among those into which the hot water was poured [choosing the purest]. These ladies wore gauze outer garments, fine silk trains, karaginu, and saishi.[1] Their hair was tied by white cords which gave the head a very fair look. In the bath Lady Saishō became the partner of bathing [i.e. enter-ed the bath with the royal infant]. Lady Dainagon in her bathing-dress—she was especially beautiful in this rare costume. The Lord Prime Minister took the August Prince in his arms ; Lady Koshōshō held the sword, and Lady Miya-no-Naishi held up a tiger's head before the Prince.[2] Lady Miya-no-Naishi wore karaginu with a pattern of pine cones. Her train was woven in a marine design of sea-weeds, waves, etc. ; on the belt a vine-pattern was embroidered. Lady Koshōshō wore an embroidered belt with a pattern of autumn leaves, butterflies and birds, which was bright with silver thread. Brocade was forbidden except for persons of high rank and they used it only for the belt. Two sons of the Prime Minister and

[1] Saishi : a kind of gold ornament with five radiating points worn on the forehead and tied on around the head. (See frontispiece.)
[2] This was to frighten away evil spirits.

Major-General Minamoto Masamichi were scattering rice in great excitement.[1] " I will make the most noise," each shouted to the other. The priest of Henchi Temple presented himself to protect the August Child. The rice hit him on his eyes and ears so he held out his fan and the young people laughed at him. The Doctor of Literature, Kurōdo Ben-no-Hironari, stood at the foot of the high corridor and read the first book of Sikki [historical records]. Twenty bow-string men twanged the bow-string to scare away evil spirits, they were ten men of the fifth, and ten men of the sixth degree [of rank] arranged in two rows. The same ceremonies of bathing were repeated in the evening. Only the Doctor of Literature was changed. Doctor Munetoki, Governor of Isé, read the Kōkyō [book on filial piety], and Takachika read a chapter of Buntei [in the Historical Records of Chinese Kings].

For seven nights every ceremony was performed cloudlessly. Before the Queen in white the styles and colours of other people's dresses appeared in sharp contrast.[2] I felt much dazzled and abashed, and did not present myself in the daytime, so I passed my days in tranquillity and watched persons going up from the eastern side building across the bridge. Those who were permitted to wear the honourable

[1] Rice-scattering ; for good luck.
[2] Here occurs an untranslatable sentence. Literally it would seem to be : *It seems hair growing in good monochromatic picture.* That might mean that the Queen seemed like a beauty in a picture drawn with ink and brush (see some illustrations in this book).

86

colours[1] put on brocaded karaginu,[2] and also brocaded uchigi. This was the conventionally beautiful dress, not showing individual taste. The elderly ladies who could not wear the honourable colours avoided anything dazzling, but took only exquisite uchigi[3] trimmed with three or five folds.[4] and for karaginu brocade either of one colour or of a simple design. For their inner kimonos they used figured stuffs or gauzes. Their fans, though not at first glance brilliant or attractive, had some written phrases or sentiments in good taste, but almost exactly alike, as if they had compared notes beforehand. In point of fact the resemblance came from their similarity of age, and they were individual efforts. Even in those fans were revealed their minds which are in jealous rivalry. The younger ladies wore much-embroidered clothes ; even their sleeve openings were embroidered. The pleats of their trains were ornamented with thick silver thread and they put gold foil on the brocaded figures of the silk. Their fans were like a

[1] Purple and scarlet.
[2] Karaginu : a short garment with long sleeves and worn of a different colour from the uchigi. (See frontispiece.)
[3] Uchigi : long unconfined flowing robe put on over the dress. It was made of elegant material and lined with another colour and was the distinctive and beautiful part of the court dress of that day. Under it were worn two or more other silk robes of different colours, one often intended to show through and modify the colour of the other. They were fastened in front by a belt like the present-day kimono, and over them was hung at the back the long and elaborate train of heavy white silk on which the last word of elegance in embroidery or painting was placed. In the presence of Royalty the ladies knelt in rows one behind the other, and doubtless these trains made a great display spread out before those sitting behind. (See frontispiece.)
[4] See frontispiece.

snow-covered mountain in bright moonlight ; they sparkled and could not be looked at steadily. They were like hanging mirrors [in those days made of polished metal].

On the third night Her Majesty's major-domo gave an entertainment. He served the Queen himself. The dining-table of aloe wood, the silver dishes, and other things I saw hurriedly. Minamoto Chūnagon and Saishō presented the Queen with some baby clothes and diapers, a stand for a clothes chest, and cloth for wrapping up clothes and furniture. They were white in colour, and all of the same shape, yet they were carefully chosen, showing the artist mind. The Governor of Ōmi Province was busy with the general management of the banquet. On the western balcony of the East building there sat court nobles in two rows, the north being the more honourable place. On the southern balcony were court officials, the west being the most honourable seat. Outside the doors of the principal building [where the Queen was] white figured-silk screens were put.

On the fifth night the Lord Prime Minister celebrated the birth. The full moon on the fifteenth day was clear and beautiful. Torches were lighted under the trees and tables were put there with rice-balls on them. Even the uncouth humble servants who were walking about chattering seemed to enhance the joyful scene. All minor officials were there burning torches, making it as bright as day. Even the atten-

88

dants of the nobles, who gathered behind the rocks and under the trees, talked of nothing but the new light which had come into the world, and were smiling and seemed happy as if their own private wishes had been fulfilled. Happier still seemed those in the Audience Chamber, from the highest nobles even to men of the fifth rank, who, scarcely to be counted among the nobility, met the joyful time going about idly, and bending their bodies busily [i.e. obsequiously].

To serve at the Queen's dinner eight ladies tied their hair with white cords, and in that dress brought in Her Majesty's dining-table. The chief lady-in-waiting for that night was Miya-no-Naishi. She was brilliantly dressed with great formality, and her hair was made more charming by the white cords which enhanced her beauty. I got a side glance of her when her face was not screened by her fan. She wore a look of extreme purity.

The following are the maids-of-honour who tied their hair; Minamoto Shikibu, daughter of the Governor of Kaga Province; Kozaémon, daughter of the late Michitoki, Governor of Bitchū; Kohyoé, daughter of Akimasa, Governor of the Left Capital; Ōsuké, daughter of Sukechika, the head priest of the Isé shrine; Ōuma, daughter of Yorinobu, an officer of the Right Bodyguard; Kouma, daughter of Michinobu, an officer of the Left Bodyguard; Kohyoé, daughter of Narichika, Recorder of the Capital; Komoku, daughter of Nobuyoshi. These were all young and pretty. It was a sight worth seeing. This time, as they chose only the best-looking young ladies, the rest who used to tie their hair on ordinary occasions to serve the Queen's dinner wept bitterly; it was shocking to see them.

More than thirty ladies were sitting in the two rooms east of the Queen's canopy, a magnificent sight. The august dinner trays were carried by unemé.[1] Near the entrance of the great chamber folding screens surrounded a pair of tables on which these dining-trays had been placed. As the night advanced the moon shone brightly. There were unemé,[1] mohitori,[2] migushiagé,[3] tonomori,[4] kanmori-no-nyokwan,[5]—some with whose faces I was not familiar. There were also doorkeepers, carelessly dressed and with hairpins falling out, crowded together towards the eastern corridor of the principal building as if it were a public holiday. There were so many people that there was no getting through them. After dinner the maids-of-honour came outside the misu and could be plainly seen by the light of the torches. The train and karaginu of Lady Ōshikibu was embroidered to represent the dwarf pine-wood at Mount Oshio. She is the wife of Michinoku, Governor of the eastern extremity of the island, and she serves now in the Prime

[1] Unemé : women selected from various provinces for their beauty, especially to wait on the Royal table.
[2] Mohitori : officials who had charge of wells, shoyu (Japanese sauce) and ice-houses.
[3] Migusiagé : attendants whose hair was done up with hairpins.
[4] King's housekeepers.　　　　　　[5] Cleaners.

90

Of Old Japan

Minister's household. Daibu-no-Miyobu neglected the ornamentation of her karaginu, but she adorned her train with silver dust representing sea-waves. It was pleasing to the eye, though not dazzling. Ben-no-Naishi showed on her train a beach with cranes on it painted in silver. It was something new. She had also embroidered pine branches ; she is clever, for all these things are emblematic of a long life. The device of Lady Shōshō was inferior to these—many laughed at her silver foil. She was sister to Suke-mitsu, the Governor of Shinano, and has lived at the court a long time. People wanted to see this entertainment. A priest was there who used to attend the court to beguile the night with religious and other stories. I said to him, " You cannot see such a lovly thing every day." " Indeed ! indeed !" said he, neglecting his Buddha and clapping his hands for joy. The court nobles rose from their seats and went to the steps [descending from the balcony]. His Lordship the Prime Minister and others cast da.[1] It was shocking to see them quarrelling about paper. Some [others] composed poems. A lady said, " What response shall we make if some one offers to drink saké with us?" We tried to think of something.[2]

[1] Da : a gambling game now not known. It was played with dice.
[2] (The following poem, then composed, is made with words of two meanings. It is impossible to arrange it in poetic form in English, but we present the two meanings in separate phrases, which the reader may combine for himself.)
Japanese words with their meanings :
    Mezurashiki hikari = uncommon light. [Continued on the next page]

Diaries of Court Ladies

Shijō-no-Dainagon is a man of varied accomplishments. No ladies can rival him in repartee, much less compete with him in poetry, so they were all afraid of him, but [this evening] he did not give a cup to any particular lady to make her compose poems. Perhaps that was because he had many things to do and it was getting late. At this ceremony the ladies of high rank are given robes, together with babies' dresses presented by the Queen. The ladies of the fourth rank were each given a lined kimono, and those of the sixth rank were given hakama.[1] So much I saw.

The next night the moon was very beautiful. As it is the delightful season, young people went boating. They were all dressed uniformly in white and their hair showed better than when they wear coloured clothes. Kodaibu, Gen-shikibu, Miyaki-no-Jiju, Gosechi-no-Ben, Ukon, Kohyoé, Koemon, Uma, Yasurahi, Isebito—these were on the veranda when the Lieutenant-General of the Left Bodyguard, and the Lieutenant-General, the Prime Minis-

Sashi sou = { added. / pour more saké into.

Sakazuki wa = { waxing moon. / a cup.

Chiyomo = for a thousand ages.

Megurame = circulate { circulate, O moon never waning! / circulate the cup to all persons coutless times.

Poem.

First meaning:

We pray that the waxing moon [i.e. the young Prince] *may never wane, but shine for a thousand ages without change!*

Second meaning:

May this cup [of joy] *be full as soon as emptied and circulate freely to all!*

[1] A pleated divided skirt worn by both men and women.

92

ter's son, came to take them out in the boat punted
by Lieutenant-General Kanetaka of the Right Bodyguard. The rest of the ladies were neglected and
followed them with their eyes. They seemed to be
jealous in spite of themselves. Into the very white
garden[1] the moon shone down and added to the
beauty of the maids-of-honour in their white dresses.
There were many koshi[2] waiting at the shelter
[for conveyances] near the north entrance. They
were those of the ladies-in-waiting of His Majesty's
court, Tōsanmi, Koshōshō, Uma, Ukon, Chikuzen,
Ōmi—so far I have heard, but as I dont' know them
well there may be some mistakes. The people in the
boat came in in confusion [hearing that visitors from
the King's Court had arrived]. The Lord Prime
Minister came out to welcome them and put them in
good humour. He seemed to be perfectly happy.
Gifts were made to them according to their rank.

On the seventh day His Majesty celebrated the
birth. His secretary and Major-General, Michimasa,
came as King's Messenger with a long list [of the
presents] put into a wicker box. A letter was immediately sent from the Queen to the King. The
students from the Kangakuin[2] came keeping step.
The list of visitors' names was presented to Her

[1] In Kyoto it used to be the custom to cover the earth of the gardens with
very white fine sand.
[2] A two-wheeled vehicle drawn by a bullock, used by noblemen and
ladies of the period.
[3] A school created in 825 A.D. by the Prime Minister Fujiwara Fuyutsugu
to educate the younger members of the Fujiwara family.

Majesty. Some may perhaps receive gifts.

The ceremony of the evening was noisier than ever. I peeped under the Queen's canopy. She who is esteemed by the people as the mother of the nation did not seem to be in good spirits. She appeared a little weary. She had grown thinner, and her appearance in bed was slenderer, younger, and gracefuller. A little lantern was hung under the canopy which chased the darkness away even from the corners. Her fair complexion was pale and transparently pure. I thought her abundant hair would be better tied up. There is great impropriety in writing about her at all, so I will stop here.

The general ceremonies were the same as the other day. The gifts to the courtiers were bestowed from within the misu. The women's dresses and the Queen's dress [perhaps from the Queen's wardrobe] were added to them. The chief of the King's secretaries and court nobles received them, approaching the misu.

His Majesty's gifts were uchigi, and kimonos, and rolls of silk in the usual court fashion.[1] The gifts to Tachibana-no-Sanmi [who offered the breast to the young Prince for the first time] were a set of women's clothes and rolls of brocade, a silver clothes chest, and wrappings for clothes [which perhaps were white]. I have heard that something wrapped up was added also, though I could not see it in detail.

On the eighth day all changed their dress [which

[1] This "court fashion" of sending rolls of silk as presents from the Emperor or Empress prevails to-day, one thousand years later.

94

had been white, the colour of purification]. On the ninth evening the Vice-Governor[1] of the August Crown Prince's retinue celebrated the birth. The present was put on a white cabinet. The ceremony was quite in the new style. On the silver clothe's chest a raised ornament was carved, and the island of Hōrai[2] was also represented as usual, but in finer and newer fashion. I am sorry I cannot describe it all exactly. This evening the winter screens were used, and the ladies wore richly coloured dresses. They seemed all the more charming as it was the first time after the birth [to see them]. The rich and brilliant colours shone through the karaginu. The women's figures also showed more distinctly and that enhanced their beauty. This was the night that Lady Koma-no-Omoto was put to shame.

It was after the tenth day of the Gods-absent month, but the Queen could not leave her bed. So night and day ladies attended her in her apartment towards the West. The Lord Prime Minister visited her both during the night and at dawn. He examined the breasts of the wet-nurses. Those nurses who were in a sound sleep were much startled and got up while still asleep ; it was quite a pity to see them. He very naturally devoted himself with the utmost care,

[1] This person was the second son of the Prime Minister ; therefore the Queen's brother or half-brother and uncle of the Crown Prince.

[2] The island of Hōrai ; Japanese Elysium, a crystal island of eternal youth and felicity, supposed to exist in mid-ocean. A miniature presentation of this island is used on festal occasions as the emblem of eternity, or unchangeableness.

while there was anxiety about the August Child. Sometimes the Honourable Infant did a very unreasonable thing and wet the Lord Prime Minister's clothes. He, loosening his sash, dried his dress behind the screen. He said: " Ah ! it is a very happy thing to be wet by the Prince. When I am drying my clothes is my most comfortable moment !" So he said rejoicing. He especially favoured Prince Murakami, and as he thinks I am related to that Prince he talked to me very familiarly. I know many things which may be expected to happen !¹

The day of the King's visit was approaching, and the Lord's mansion was improved and adorned. Beautiful chrysanthemums were sought for everywhere, to plant in the garden. Some were already fading, others in yellow were especially lovely. When they were planted and I saw them through the shifting morning mists, they seemed indeed to drive away old age.

I wish I could be more adaptable and live more gaily in the present world—had I not an extraordinary sorrow—but whenever I hear delightful or interesting things my yearning for a religious life grows stronger. I become melancholy and lament. I try to forget, for sorrow is vain. Am I too sinful? So I was musing one morning when I saw waterfowl playing heedlessly in the pond.²

¹ The Prime Minister wished to arrange a marriage between his eldest son and the Prince's daughter. The authoress's cousin had adopted the Prince's son.

² This incident has for some reason become very famous and artists

Of Old Japan

Waterfowl floating on the water—
They seem so gay,
But in truth
It is not gay to live anxiously seeking means of existence.

I sympathized with them who outwardly have no other thought but amusememt, yet in reality are seeking a livelihood in great anxiety.

Lady Koshōshō sent me a letter, and when I was writing the answer a brisk shower came pattering down. The sky looked threatening and the messenger was in a hurry, so I think I wrote but a broken-legged poem. After dark the messenger returned with a strongly perfumed and deeply coloured paper[1] on which was written :

> *The dark sky dulls my dreamy mind,*
> *The down-dripping rain lingers —*
> *O my tears down falling, longing after thee !*

I have forgotten what I wrote to her except the poem:

> *There are pauses between the showers of the outer world,*
> *But there is no time when my sleeves, wet with tears, are dry.*

That day the Queen saw the new boats which were presented for her inspection. The dragon's head and the phœnix at the prow made me think of animated living figures.

have used it as a subject for pictures. One of these is now hanging in the Imperial Museum in Tokyo.
[1] Poems were written on oblongs of crimson, yellow, gold, or other paper according to the feeling of the writer. Nowadays oblong poem papers can be bought anywhere, but they are generally white or gray with gold decoration.

The visit[1] of His Majesty was to be made at eight or nine o'clock in the morning. From early dawn ladies adorned themselves with great care. As the seats of the courtiers were placed in the west side building the Queen's apartment was not so much disturbed. I have heard that the ladies serving at the Imperial shrine dressed very elaborately in the rooms of the first maid-of-honour.

In the early morning Lady Koshōshō came back from her father's. We dressed our hair together. In spite of the fixed hour His Majesty's coming will be delayed, we thought, and our relaxed minds were still indolent. Some ladies had ordered unornamented silk fans and were on tiptoe with expectancy when the drums were heard [announcing Royalty] and they were in an awkward predicament.[2] We welcomed the Royal equipage. The boatmen's music was very good. When the Royal koshi drew near, the bearers, though they were rather honourable persons, bent their heads in absolute humility as they ascended the steps. Even in the highest society there are grades of courtesy, but these men were too humble. The Royal dais was prepared at the west side of the Queen's.[3] His honourable chair was placed in the eastern part of the south veranda. A little apart from it on the east side were hung misu, and two of the court ladies in attendance on the King came out from

---

[1] The King's visit was made October 16, 1008.

[2] It was *de rigueur* for ladies to conceal their faces with fans.

[3] The left side is the more honourable position, but this time the King sat at the right side because perhaps they could not move the Queen's dais.

behind that misu. The beautiful shape of their hair, tied with bands, was like that of the beauties in Chinese pictures. Lady Saémon held the King's sword. She wore a blue-green patternless karaginu and shaded train with floating bands and belt of " floating thread" brocade dyed in dull red. Her outer robe was trimmed with five folds and was chrysanthemum-coloured. The glossy[1] silk was of crimson ; her figure and movement, when we caught a glimpse of it, was flower-like and dignified. Lady Ben-no-Naishi held the box of the King's seals. Her uchigi was grape-coloured, her brocaded train and karaginu were the same as the former lady. She is a very small and smile-giving person and seemed a little shy and I was sorry for her. Her face and clothes were in better taste than those of the other ladies. Her hair-bands were blue-green. Her appearance suggested one of the ancient dream-maidens descended from heaven.

The officers of the King's Bodyguard managed things connected with the state carriage [perhaps drawn by a bullock] in fine style. They were elegantly dressed. The First Lieutenant-General took His Majesty's sword and gave it to Lady Saémon.

Looking over those who were inside the misu I saw that persons who were permitted to wear honourable colours were in karaginu of blue or red, painted trains, and uchigi which were as a rule brocade of old red and old rose. Only the Right Bodyguard wore

[1] A special effect of brilliant shining produced by beating the silk.

clothes of shrimp pink. The beaten[1] stuffs were like the mingling of dark and light maple leaves in autumn. The under garments were in deep and pale jasmine yellow or in green and white. Some wore scarlet and green, and others dresses trimmed with three folds. Among those who were not permitted to wear figured silk the elderly persons wore blue, or dull red and old rose five-fold-bordered uchigi. The colour of the sea painted on their trains was tasteful and quiet. On their belts was a repeated design.

The younger ladies wore five-fold-trimmed karaginu of chrysanthemum colours according to their taste. The first garment was white and those who wore a blue dress covered it with a red one. Those who wore old rose on the outside took more richly coloured garments underneath.[2] Among those whose dress was in combination with white, only those who made skilful combinations seemed well dressed. I saw some fans exquisitely strange and original. We can compare their tastes more easily in their everyday dress, but on such an occasion as this, when they give their whole minds to the costumes, vying with each other, they all seem like so many works of art. They look rather alike, and it is difficult to distinguish ages, or to know whether hair is thick or thin. Their faces and heads were hidden by fans, yet some ladies seemed more dignified and others inferior.

[1] A special effect of brilliant shining produced by beating the silk.

[2] These garments were evidently made of very thin material, colours underneath being intended to modify the outer ones, hence the art of dressing became very subtle.

Ladies who seem distinguished at such a time must be beautiful indeed. Five ladies who had formerly served both the King and our Queen were assembled here. They were, two ladies-in-waiting, two maids-of-honour, and one cook.[1]

To serve the dinner Ladies-in-Waiting Chikuzen and Sakyō, their hair tied with bands, came out near the square pillar where the court ladies sat. They were like beautiful angels [Japanese word, ten-nin]. Sakyō wore karaginu of white, and blue under white. Lady Chikuzen wore five-fold-trimmed karaginu of chrysanthemum colours. The ornament of their trains was dyed by rubbing.[2] Lady Tachibana of the Third Rank prepared the dinner. She is an old lady and wore blue[3] karaginu, and yellow chrysanthemum uchigi woven in a "floating thread" pattern. A sudare was rolled up, but a post obscured the view. The Lord Prime Minister, taking the August young Prince in his arms went before the King. His Majesty took the child himself. The Honourable Infant cried a little in a very young voice. Lady Ben-no-Saishō stood holding the Prince's sword. The Prince was taken to the Lord Prime Minister's

[1] Doubtless this office was highly important and held in honour. In those days poison and inferior foods were to be guarded against. Through out the journal it may be noticed that all directly serving the King and Queen in any way are persons of high rank.

[2] In this curiously delicate operation the actual leaf or flower from which the colour was obtained was rubbed onto the silk to make the desired pattern.

[3] Light blue and some kinds of yellow are colours relegated to the elderly in Japan. Babies and young people are dressed in bright colours and showy patterns. The old wear plain stuffs and pale or dull colours.

Diaries of Court Ladies

wife, who sat on the west side of the inner door. After His Majesty had gone, Ben-no-Saishō came out and said to me : " I was exposed to brightness [i.e. the radiance of the King's presence]. I felt discomposed." Her blushing face was beautiful in every feature, and set off her dress delightfully.

When night came we had beautiful dances. The court nobles presented themselves before the King [to dance]. The names of the dances performed were :
The Pleasures of Ten Thousand Ages.
The Pleasures of a Peaceful Reign.
The Happy Palace.
When they danced the " Long-Pleasing[1] Son," the closing one, they went out singing and danced along the road beyond the garden hills.[2]   As they went farther away the sound of flute and drum mingled with the sound of wind in the pine-wood towards which they were going. The garden brook, cleansed very carefully, was refreshing to us and the [sound of the] water rippling on the pond gave us a chilly feeling. Lady Sakyo offered the Queen sympathy, not knowing that she had doubled her undergarments, so people laughed secretly. Lady Chikuzen talked of the late King Enyu,[3] who had visited this residence often. She talked about the events of those days, and I felt that

[1] This dance was performed by court nobles at the coronation of the late Emperor Taishō at Kyoto, 1915.
[2] Artificial hills in Japanese gardens are intended to bring mountain scenery to mind, whether large or small. They are sometimes of considerable size.
[3] Reigned 970 to 984. This old lady may have served him and had

she was about to utter things unfit for this happy occasion, so I did not answer her saying I was too tired. We were sitting with a curtain between us. If there had been some one to ask, "Alas, what things?" she would have spilled the unfit words. The dancing before the King had begun and it was very delightful, when the voice of the young Prince was heard crying beautifully. The Minister of the Right said flatteringly that the August Child's voice was in accord with the music. The Commander of the King's Left Bodyguard recited with others " The Pleasures of Ten Thousand Years " and " The Pleasures of Ten Thousand Autumns." Our honourable host, the Lord Prime Minister, said, " Ah ! I held the previous condescending visit as a great honour, but this is the greatest." He wept in intoxication of joy. There's really no need of my saying it, but he is so grateful to the King and so conscious of his happiness. It is lovely to see it.

The Prime Minister withdrew and His Majesty retired from the chamber. He summoned the Minister of the Right to order him to record that the Queen's officials and Prime Minister's stewards were to be advanced in rank. Tō-no Ben presented to him all who were to be thus honoured. The nobles of the Fujiwara clans[1] arrived together, but there were interesting reminiscences to relate.

[1] The feuds of the Fujiwara family. Fujiwara Fuhito had four sons who became the founders of the four great Fujiwara families—Minami, Kyo, Kita, and Shiki. They were all aspiring to the King's favour and at enmity with each other, the present Prime Minister Michinaga far outstripping the others in power.

only those immediately connected with the Prime Minister's family, the other three families were not among them. Then came the chief officers of the Right Bodyguard, the high officials of the Queen Dowager, the officials of our Queen to whom additional duties were assigned, and other members of the court who had been promoted and who came to thank the King. His Majesty went in beside the Queen, but as the night was far advanced it was not long before the Prime Minister called the Royal carriage and the King returned to his own palace.

The next day Royal messengers came here before the morning mist had cleared up. I arose late and did not see them. Last evening was the first time that His Majesty the King had met the Queen during these months. After the visit the duties of the August Prince's attendants and ladies were made public. Some who had not heard about it before were disappointed and jealous. The decorations of the Queen's apartment, which had been neglected, were improved. Things became more attractive in the Queen's presence. For years the Prime Minister had felt anxious [as the Queen had had no child], but his hopes being realized he and his wife devoted themselves to taking care of the Queen. The August Child seems to have shed brightness around him.

In the evening the moonlight was very beautiful. The Second Official of the August young Prince came, perhaps thinking that his thanks might be offered by

a court lady. The bridge opposite the door was wet
with vapour from the bath. No one answered, so he
went to the room of Lady Miya-no-Naishi which is
next the bridge of the eastern building. Lady Saishō
was in the inner room. The man, holding back the
unlocked door, asked again, " Is some one within ?"
But she did not come out. Just then the Queen's
First Officer appeared and called, " Is some one
there ?" She felt it impossible not to reply, so made
a faint answer. The new official was in a gay humour
and said reproachfully, " You did not answer me,
but you especially favour the Head Officer ! It is
natural enough, but not kind ; is there so much
difference between the nobles in this place ? It is too
much !" He sung " The August Happiness of the
Day." As the night advanced the moon became
brighter ; " It would be better to take away the
obstruction from before the door," said he persua-
sively. I thought it awkward that a noble of the
Court should stand there below me like that, but I
did not open the door. If I were younger, I thought,
my inexperience would be my excuse were I to talk
with him or open the door, but one cannot talk
thoughtlessly when one is young no longer, so I did
not open the door but held it with my hand.

The first day of the Frost month was the fiftieth
day after the birth. The persons who were to present themselves came in full dress. The sight before
her presence was like a picture of a poet's assembly.
Many kichō were arranged along the east side of the

Queen's dais feom the inner room to the veranda.
The Royal dining-table was placed towards the south
front of the house. At the west side was prepared
the Queen Dowager's dinner. It was placed on a
tray of aloe wood. I don't know what kind of a stand
it was on because I did not see it. She wore a grape-
coloured kimono trimmed with five folds and red
uchigi. Those serving the dinner were Lady Saishō
and Lady Sanuki. The maids-of-honour dressed
their hair with saishi and bands. Lady Dainagon
served the August Prince's dinner at the east side—
a little dining-table, plate, stand for chopsticks, with
a central decoration representing a bit of seashore—
all as small as playthings for dolls. At the east end
where the sudaré was a little rolled up, there were
in waiting such ladies as Ben-no-Naishi, Lady Nakatsukasa, Lady Koshōshō ; as I was inside I could not
see in great detail. That night Lady Shō, the nurse,
was permitted to wear a dress of honourable colour.
She seemed still girlish, as she took the August Prince
in her arms and gave him to the Lord Prime Minister
who was within the dais. He came out quietly and
they were plainly seen in the flickering light of the
torches. It was very lovely. The August Prince
was dressed in red brocade with shaded skirt—exquisitely pretty. The mochi[1] was given to him by the
Lord Prime Minister. The seats of the courtiers had
been prepared at the west side of the east building ;
there were two ministers present. They came out
to the bridge and were very drunk and boisterous.

[1] Mochi : a cake made of beaten rice flour paste.

106

As the torches burnt low, the Major-General of the
Fourth Rank was called to light lanterns. Boxes and
baskets of food,[1] the Prime Minister's gifts, were
borne in by the attendants and piled up on the balcony near the railing. Some of the boxes were to be
taken to the King's kitchen, and as the next day was
to be a day of abstinence for religious devotion they
were carried away at once.

The Queen's First Officer came to the misu and
asked if the court nobles should be invited there. As
the answer was " yes," every one came led by the
Prime Minister, and approached the east door. Ladies stood in two or three rows ; the misu was rolled
up by those who were nearest it, Lady Dainagon,
Lady Koshōshō, and others. The Minister of the
Right came dancing wildly and made a hole in the
kichō behind which ladies were sitting. They laughed, saying, " He has long passed the age for that."
He did not notice, but made a great many unbecoming jokes, taking away ladies' fans. The August
Prince's First Officer took a saké cup[2] and stepped
out ; he sung a song ; although it was unaccompa-
nied by dancing it was very delightful. Farther
towards the east, leaning against a door-post, the

[1] These dainty white wooden boxes of food arranged in a way pleasing to
the eye are still a feature of Japanese life. They are distributed, with
varying contents, at weddings and funerals, sold at railway stations, and
carried on picnics.

[2] At banquets a great cup was used which could contain one or two
quarts of liquor. When this was circulated among the guests each was
expected to empty the cup, and it was the pride of the drinker to toss it off
in one draught.

General of the Right was standing, studying the
ladies' sleeves and the skirts of their garments showing below the misu.   He is different from other men.
The ladies, thinking that after all the intoxicated men
were only trying to seem young and irresistible, made
light of their behavior and said, "It is nothing,
nobody else will behave so."   Compared with such
men the General is far superior.   He was afraid of the
saké cup, and when it came to him passed it by,
singing the song which begins "One Thousand and
Ten Thousand Ages," The First Officer of the
Light Bodyguard said, "I think Lady Murasaki[1] must
be somewhere here!"   I listened, thinking, "How
can she be here in a place where there is no such
graceful person as Prince Genji?"[2] The Minister of
the Right said, "Sanmi-no-Suké [officer of the third
rank], accept this cup!"   When the officer came out
from below the Lord Keeper of the seal [an inferior
position] the drunken man wept.   The King's Adviser, leaning in a corner, was flirting with Lady
Hyobu.   The Prime Minister did not forbid even
unmentionable jokes.   It was an awful night of
carousal, so after the ceremony I signalled to Lady
Saishō and we hid ourselves, but there came noisily
the Prime Minister's sons and Lieutenant-General
Saishō, so, although we two had remained hidden
behind the screen, even this was taken away and we
were captives.   "Compose a poem each, and you
shall be excused," said the Lord Prime Minister.   I

[1] The young heroine of Genji Monogatari.
[2] The hero of Genji Monogatari.

was frightened and helpless, and made haste to comply :

How can I number the years of the Prince !
One thousand, nay, eight thousand, may he live, and more.

" Well done !" said he, reciting it twice, and he answered immediately :

O would I might live the life of a crane—
Then might I reckon the years of the Prince
Up to one thousand !

He was much intoxicated, but the poem had feeling, for it came from his innermost desire. The child cherished in this way will have a very bright future. Even such as I can imagine the thousand prosperous years of His August Highness ! He felt satisfied with his own poem and said, " Has Your Majesty heard the poem ? I have made a poem !" and then—" I am worthy to be your father and you are worthy to be my daughter—Mother is smiling, she must think she is happy. She may be thinking she has got a good husband !" said he in extreme intoxication. As is usual with drunken persons all were listening. His wife seemed to be embarrassed by this conversation and retired. " Mother will be angry if I do not follow her," said he, and went through the dais hurriedly muttering, " Excuse me, Your Majesty, but a child is adored because of its father !" and everybody laughed.

The day for the Queen's return to the palace approaches and her ladies have no tranquil hours because of continual ceremonies. Her Majesty had had blank books made, so from early morning I was summoned to attend her to arrange the paper and to write letters which were sent with the books and the romances to be copied. I also spent days in compiling these into books. "What fancy is this? Why do you do such things these chilly days?" the Lord Prime Minister said, but he himself brought out fine papers, brushes and ink, and even writing-boxes. These were given to the ladies by the Queen's own hand. They were bashful, but excuses were in vain, and they went into corners and composed and came back blushing, saying, "I have done this," only to be given more brushes and ink. I had brought my romances from home and hidden them in my own room, but one day the Prime Minister entered it secretly to hunt about and found them and gave them to the first lady-in-waiting. As the books are not at all clearly written, I am ashamed to think what their opinion must be.[1]

The infant Prince begins to babble and crow. His Majesty is naturally impatient to have him. The waterfowl have begun to come more and more to the pond before the house.

I longed for snow while we were staying there, but just then I had to go home to my parents. Two days after retiring from the Court a great snow came. The old familiar trees of my home reminded me of those

[1] The Queen desired a literary Court to rival that of the first Queen. See note on p. 131.

melancholy years when I used to gaze upon them musing when the colours of flowers, the voices of birds, the skies of spring and autumn, moon shadows, frost and snow, told me nothing but that time was revolving, and that I was menaced with a dreary future. Before I went to Court I tried to avoid sadness by writing to those who were in the same state of mind, even to those with whom I was only slightly acquainted, and associating with them I consoled my heart in various ways. Although an unimportant person I had passed my life without feeling any sort of contempt of myself until I went to Court—since then, alas! I have experienced all the bitterness of it. To-day I took out romances, but they no longer interested me. I was ashamed to think what those melancholy persons to whom I used to write had thought of me since I went to Court, so I had no courage to write to them again. Those with whom I am now intimate would have to publish my letters broadcast, so how can I write to them my inmost heart?—thus my letters have inadvertently grown few. I had a feeling that association with some of the younger ladies who used to visit me before I went to Court could not continue. Some of them I had to refuse when they came, and in my home all these trifles have made me feel more deeply that I have gone into a world not intended for me. I write only to those from whom I can never part, to whom my heart prompts me to speak. O worthless heart, that feels love only for those with whom it daily associates! I long for Lady Dainagon with whom I spent every night before the

Queen, when we told each other all our heart's secrets
—is it also my worldly heart that longs for a companion other than Buddha?

> *Like two wild ducks*
> *Floating with unrestful slumber,*
> *Yet even those nights I would recall—*
> *Feathers wet and cold—*
> *But colder tears!*

Lady Dainagon returned this answer:

> *Midnight sleep was broken*
> *But no friend to brush away the cold tears!*
> *I envy the Oshidori*[1] *which has ever its mate by its side.*

Her handwriting is very elegant. She is a very true-hearted person.

A lady wrote me, " The Queen has seen the snow, and she regrets deeply that you are not here at Court." The Prime Minister's Lady wrote to me, " When I tried to stop your going away you said you would go at once that you might come back soon. Was not that true?—for many days have passed." She may not have been in earnest, yet as I received such a letter I went back to the Court.

It was on the seventeenth of the Frost month that the Queen went back to the palace. The time had been fixed for eight o'clock in the evening, but the night was far advanced. I could not see more than thirty ladies who tied up their hair. To the east

[1] A special kind of wild duck called oshidori which is always seen in couples.

A NOBLEMAN'S KOSHI

balcony of the Queen's apartments came more than
ten ladies-in-waiting from His Majesty's Court [to
escort the Queen]. Her Majesty's senji [woman who
repeats the Queen's words to outsiders] went in Her
Majesty's coach with her. The Lord Prime Minister's
wife and Lady Shō, the nurse, holding the August
Infant in her arms, went in a coach adorned with silk
fringes. Lady Dainagon and Lady Saishō were in a
gold-studded coach. In the next one went Lady Koshōshō and Lady Miya-no-Naishi. The Lieutenant-
General of His Majesty's steed was in the next one. I
was to go in that one. His manner expressed dis-
satisfaction with so mean a companion and I was
much discomposed. Lady Jiyū, Ben-no-Naishi, Lady
Saemon, the Prime Minister's first attendant, and Lady
Shikibu went in their proper order in their koshis.
As it was in bright moonlight I was greatly
embarrassed, and in the palace I followed the Lieutenant-General not knowing where I trod. If some
one had been *looking at me from behind* [Japanese
expression signifying " gossiping about or criticiz-
ing "], I must have been ashamed indeed.

I passed that night in the third little room on the
corridor of the Kokiden.[1] Lady Koshōshō came and
we talked of the sadness of our lives. We took off
our kimonos and put on doubly wadded ones, and
making a fire in an incense-burner we were complaining of the cold when the Chamberlain and the

[1] Kokiden : residence of the first Queen.

Diaries of Court Ladies

State Councillor and Lieutenant-General Kinnobu came to inquire for us. I wished I might have been entirely forgotten this evening. It annoyed more than it pleased us; nevertheless, as they had come to make inquiries, I said : " To-morrow I will return the compliment and go to inquire after you. To-night I am shivering with cold." Saying these words we secretly stole away from that room. Some were now preparing to go back to their homes ; we thought them to be some of the lower officials. I do not say this as comparing them with myself. By the way, Lady Koshōshō is very noble in character and beautiful, but I notice she is thinking sadly of the World.[1] One reason is her father's rather humble rank which makes good fortune delay to come to her.

This morning Her Majesty saw in detail last evening's presents from the Prime Minister. The hair ornaments in a case were more lovely than words can express. There were a pair of salvers. On one of them were poem papers and bound blank books. On the other were the poetical collections of the Kokinshū, Gosenshū, and Jūishū.[2] Each was bound in five volumes. The copyists of these volumes were the King's Adviser and attendant of middle rank and Enkwan.[3] The covers were of thin figured silk ; the fastenings of braided silk of the same material.

[1] The World ; i.e. matrimonial affairs.
[2] Three anthologies, of Ancient and Modern Poems, Later Selections of Poems, and Miscellaneous Poems, respectively.
[3] These men were famous calligraphers.

114

Of Old Japan

They were fitted into a basket. There were also ancient and modern poetical collections of various families, such as those of Yoshinobu and Motosuké. The copies made by Enkwan[1] and Chikazumi[2] were kept for the Queen's private use. They were made in the new fashion.

On the twentieth day of the Frost month the dance of Gosechi[3] was performed. A costume was given to the young lady whom the King's attendant and State Councillor offered for the dance. The Lieutenant-General asked for a garland for his dancer, which was given. At the same time a box of perfume ornamented with artificial leaves and plum plossoms was given her. As the arrangements had been made a long time beforehand this year, there was great rivalry among the dancers. Torches were lighted in close rows along the outer doors of the eastern veranda so there was day-brightness, and it was really awkward to walk there. I felt for the girls, but it was not they only who were embarrassed. Young nobles looked at the girls face to face, almost bring-

---

[1-2] These men were famous calligraphers.

[3] This famous dance, whose origin is given below, was performed at the present Emperor's coronation at Kyoto, by five daughters of ancient noble families selected for their beauty. It is said that these young ladies immediately thereafter received a great many offers of marriage.

Gosetchi was a great holiday succeeded by two days of feasting. The dancing girls (of the diary) were all daughters of persons of high rank, three being daughters of courtiers and two daughters of province governors. Tradition says that when King Temmu was at his palace of Yoshino, heavenly maidens came down and danced before him fluttering the long celestial sleeves of their feathery dresses five times. This was the origin of the dance.

ing the lights down in front of them. They tried to draw a curtain before themselves, but in vain, and the nobles' eyes were still on them. My heart throbs even at the memory of it.

The helpers[1] of courtier Naritō's daughter were dressed in brocaded karaginu, which was distinctive and pleasing even at night. She was overwhelmed by her dress and her movements were ungraceful, yet the nobles paid her special attention. The King came to see the dance. The Lord Prime Minister, too, crept in from the side entrance, so we felt constraint.

The helpers of Nakakiyo's daughter were all of the same height. They were graceful and charming, and people agreed that they were not inferior to any ladies.

The State Councillor and Lieutenant-General had all his maids as helpers of his daughter. One of them was ungraceful, being fat and countrified, so all were laughing at her. The daughter of Tō [State Councillor] gave a fresh and distinct impression because of her family.[2] She had ten helpers.

The ladies who were proud of their good looks seemed more beautiful in this artificial light.

On the morning of the day of the Tiger[3] the courtiers assembled. Although it is a common custom to have the dance, the younger ones were especially

[1] Each dancer was attended by helpers who were sometimes persons of degree. Their duties were to arrange trains and costumes in the postures of the dance.

[2] Her father was Keeper of the Seal. Her aunt was one of the queens.

[3] See signs of the zodiac, of Old Japan.

116

curious to see the dancers. Was it because they had acquired rude country manners during these months of absence from the Court? There the dress dyed by rubbing the leaves of the indigo plant was not to be seen. When night came the second official of the Crown Prince was summoned and perfumes were bestowed upon him. Quantities of it were heaped up in a large box.

That night the dance was performed in the Seiryo-den.[1] The Queen was present to see it. The Prime Minister's wife sent a messenger to the Governor of Owari.

As the August young Prince was to be present, rice was thrown to keep off evil spirits, and people reviled them [the spirits] and called them names. It gave us a queer feeling. I was weary and wanted to rest a lit-tle, so I remained in our chamber thinking to present myself when it should be necessary. Lady Kohyoé and Lady Kohyobu sat beside the brazier. We were saying that the hall was crowded and nothing could be seen distinctly, when the Lord Prime Minister came in. " Why do you stay here? Come with us!" so we went reluctantly. I watched the dancers thinking how tired they must be, and what a heavy task they had before them. The daughter of the Governor of Owari became ill and retired. Human fate is like a dream, it seems! After the dance His Majesty retired.

[1] The name of the main building in the Imperial Palace, where the Mikado usually lives.

Young noblemen talk of nothing these days but the rooms of those dancers.[1] Even the borders of the curtains hanging over the sudaré were varied according to the taste of the dancer. Their hair-dressing and their style also varied extremely, so the young men talked about that, and more improper things too. Even in ordinary years [when there was no unusual festivity] the dancing girls' hearts are always filled with anxiety, how much more so this year. While I was thinking about it they came out in single file. My heart swelled with sympathy. It may be they have no great patrons to depend on who could protect them. As they are all chosen for their beauty all are attractive, and it would be difficult to say which is superior to the other, although the man of fashion may perhaps perceive differences. In this brilliant light they may not even shade their faces with their fans. They are placed in rivalry with each other in rank, in prudence, and in wit, and must struggle each to excel the other, although at the same time they feel shyness in the presence of the young men. Surrounded by the young nobles, they are forced to hold their own among them worthily. I feel sorry for them.

Governor Tamba's daughter wore a darkish blue gown. The State Councillor Tō's daughter wore red. The maids of the latter wore the blue karaginu of a girl and were so beautiful that they made us women

---

[1] Like the knights' tents in the tournaments each girl's apartment was distinguished by special devices of cloths or banners hung before it.

118

jealous. One girl did not seem at all dignified. The daughter of the State Councillor and Lieutenant-General was tall and had beautiful hair. Her attendants wore deep-coloured clothes trimmed with five folds and their outer garments were varied according to taste. The last girl wore a plain grape-coloured one, and that simple dress was more beautiful, as it showed taste in colour combination.

The secretaries of the sixth rank went towards them to take away their fans. They threw them down themselves. Though they were graceful they did not seem like girls. If we were in their places it would seem like a dream to us. I had never supposed I should mingle with these court ladies ! Yet the human heart is an invisible and dreadful being. If I became accustomed to [court life] my bashfulness would be overcome and I could easily stand face to face with men. As if in a vision my future appeared to me, and such a state of things appeared to me undesirable. My mind was greatly troubled and I could observe nothing.

The apartment temporarily given to the dancer who was the daughter of the King's Adviser and State Councillor was just across the way [in the building of another queen, see map of palace] on the corridor opposite to that of our Queen. A part of the sudaré of that room was in sight above the outer shutter, although we could hear voices but faintly. The State Councillor and Lieutenant-General, who knew about it all, said, " There are ladies called Sa-

119

kyō and Uma who once served that Queen over there."
" It was Sakyō who sat in the eastern part of the hall
last night as a helper of a certain young lady who
danced," askd Genshosho, who knew her. Some
of our Queen's ladies chanced to overhear these
remarks. " How extraordinary ! Yet she must
remember old times," said they ; " how is it possible
that a former lady-in-waiting should return to the
court as a maid ? She may be thinking it will never
be known, but we will one day bring it to light !"
Our ladies may have been scheming for this when
they chose among the multitude of fans kept by the
Queen those representing the Island of Hōrai[1]—did
she feel it, I wonder ?

Ground-pine [Lycopodium] was made into a
wreath and put into a box-cover [probably of a writing-box, in those days large and elegantly lacquered].
A comb and face-powder were put in also, for the
young courtiers had said, " that lady, who is rather
advanced in years, wears a curved comb suitable for
a young lady." So the comb which was put into the
box was curved too much in the vulgar new fashion
with perfume balls clumsily covered with paper. A
poem was added to it written by Lady Taifu :

Among the many ladies that night of the dance
The belle was the one who wore the lycopodium.

The Queen said : " If you are going to send at all,

[1] Hōrai : an island of eternal life and felicity supposed to exist in the
eastern ocean. Hōrai symbolizes changelessness, and it must have been
intended as a hint at the impropriety of Sakyō's changed position.

send something clever, here are many fans for it."
But some ladies replied : " That will attract too
much attention. It is too unusual. If you send this
publicly you will not succeed in puzzling her; perhaps we would better send it anonymously." Therefore a lady who was an entire stranger to her was
chosen. She went, and, speaking loudly, said :
" Here is a letter from Lady Chūnagon. It is sent
by her Queen to Lady Sakyō." I thought it would
be awkward if the messenger were caught by them,
but she ran away as soon as she had put down the
things. She reported that she heard some one saying,
" Whence do you come ?" There is no doubt she
really thought it a gift from our Queen.

Days passed without any interesting events. After that evening of dancing the Court became abso-
lutely dull. The preparatory music on the eve of the
Omi ceremony[1] was very fine. The young courtiers
were still filled with thoughts of the dancers.
After the Queen's return to the palace, the sons of
another wife of the Prime Minister were permitted to
come in to play with the ladies-in-waiting. They
came to us without end, which was a great bother.
I did not show myself to them, taking advantage of
my advanced age. They were not thinking of the
dancers, but were playing by the side of Ladies Yasu-
rai and Kohyoé, joking and chattering like little birds.

[1] Festival of the ancient gods, for which preparation was made the day
before by fasting.

At the mid-winter festival of the Kamo shrine the
Vice-Lieutenant-General [first son of the Prime
Minister] was made the King's substitute. It was a
day of fasting also, so the Lord Prime Minister had
passed the night at the palace. The nobles and dancers passed the night of the festival in making a great
noise with much merriment in the corridors. Next
morning an attendant of the Chamberlain brought
something to an attendant of the Lord Prime Minister. It was the box-cover of the previous night.[1]
There was in it a silver case for romances, besides a
mirror, a comb of aloe wood, and a silver kōgai.
The comb seemed to be given to adorn the hair of
the messenger at the festival. Something was written
on the box-cover in cursive style in raised characters.
It was the answer to the poem of the lycopodium. Two
characters were omitted and it was difficult to read.
She seemed to have misunderstood. The Chamberlain thought it really was a gift to her from our
Queen, so the return was made thus openly. It was
but a foolish joke and I felt sorry for her.

The Prime Minister's wife came to court to see the
festival. His son, adorning his head with artificial
wisteria, appeared quite a man, noble and dignified.
The Lady Kura [his nurse], not taking any notice of

[1] This incident was very well known and is mentioned in several of the
writings of the period. The mirror is the symbol of the soul of a Japanese
woman. With the mirror Sakyō sent a poem :
Alas ! the waving moss deceived your vision.
The clear mirror is never tarnished :
Therefore look deep.

the dancers, wept for joy watching her young lord. As it was still the day of fasting, they came back from the shrine at two in the morning, and the sacred dance was performed listlessly, as the important persons were absent. Kanetoki [a dancer] who had been very handsome last year, was much fallen off. Though a stranger to him I felt regret, being reminded of the fleeting life of us all.

[Here an interval occurs.]

On the twentieth of the Finishing month I went again to Court. It was the anniversary of the day on which I had first come. I remembered my former career as a wanderer on dream paths, and I loathed myself for having become so familiar with court life. The night was far advanced and as the Queen was fasting, we did not present ourselves before her. I felt lonely and was lying down. The maids-of-honour around me said : " The hours here are very different from those at home. There all would be sleeping by this time, but here our dreams are broken by the sound of shoes along the corridor." Hearing them girlishly talking I murmured to myself :

My life and the year are closing together.
At the sound of the wind dreary is my heart.

On that moon-hidden night [last night of the year] the driving off of evil spirits was soon finished. We dyed our teeth [black], and after finishing decorating our faces we sat at ease. Ben-no-Naishi came, and after talking she went to sleep. The Queen's seamstress sat in the doorway watching the maid Ateki sewing. Just then we heard an unusual noise from the direction of Her Majesty's apartment. I tried to wake up Ben-no-Naishi, but she was heavy with sleep. Some one was heard crying wildly. I was frightened and could not think what to do. Was it a fire ? But no, it was not that. I pushed the seamstress forward, saying, " Go there! over there ! Oh, dear ! " Then, " Her Majesty is in her own room, we must by all means get to her !" I shook Ben-no-Naishi roughly to awaken her and we three ran trembling—flying rather than walking. We saw two naked persons. They were Lady Yugei and Lady Kohyoé. It seemed that they had been robbed of their clothes, and I felt more distressed than before. The kitchen servants had all gone out ; even the Queen's guards had retired after devil-driving. We clapped our hands, but no one came. Some went to call the women attendants, while I, forgetting my shyness, said, " Call Hyobu-no-Jō, and the secretary." They were sought for, but had left the palace. I felt irritated indeed, but at last an assistant to the Master of Ceremonies came who poured oil into several lamps. We found many who had fainted. At the news a messenger arrived from the King, but we were too frightened to receive him properly. He took out dresses from the royal wardrobe to give them. The new dresses for New Year's Day were not stolen, so these ladies took their misfortune lightly—but unforgettably dreadful is a nude form. I can never call it laughable.

It was too dreadful to speak of, but we could not help talking.

The New Year's Day [1008] was inauspicious. The rice-cake [mochi[1]] ceremony was deferred. However, on the third day, the August Crown Prince went up to the King and the rice-cake festival was given for him. His attendant was Lady Dainagon. The dress of the ladies on the first day was karaginu of purple and old rose colour, red kimono and shaded train; on the second day, red and purple brocade, deep violet glossy silk, green karaginu, train dyed by rubbing flowers. On the third day we wore white and rose-coloured brocaded garments, trimmed with many folds. The karaginu was of dull red and old rose brocade. When we wear deep violet-coloured shining silk the inner robe is of crimson; when we wear crimson outside the inner dress is usually of deep violet. The pale and deep colour of spring leaf buds, dull red, golden yellow, and light and dark crimsons—dresses of these ordinary colours were worn trimmed with six folds in very beautiful combinations.[2]

Lady Saishō held the August Prince's honourable sword. The Lord Prime Minister took the August Prince in his arms and they presented themselves be-

---

[1] Mochi: it is still the custom in Japan to serve a cake made of beaten rice on New Year's Day, the great festival of the year. The sound of this beating is heard from house to house throughout the country, and gives everybody a holiday feeling. The ceremonies last three days.

[2] These colour combinations were very subtle because the effect was produced by the play of one or perhaps two colours showing through one another.

Diaries of Court Ladies

fore the King. Lady Saishō's dress was a garment trimmed with three and five folds, and figured of the same colour trimmed with seven folds. The uchigi was adorned with a pattern of oak-leaves beautifully embroidered. She wore a karaginu and train trimmed with three folds. Her unlined inner kimono was woven in a pattern. Her costume was in the Chinese style. Her hair was ornamented more elaborately than usual. Her style of dress and manner showed great knowledge of the world. She is rather tall and has a well-rounded figure. Her face is very small and exquisitely tinted.

[The following eleven paragraphs are portraits of prominent ladies of the court.]

LADY DAINAGON is very small and refined, white, beautiful, and round, though in demeanour very lofty. Her hair is three inches longer than her height. She uses exquisitely carved hairpins. Her face is lovely, her manners delicate and charming.

LADY SENJI is also a little person, and haughty. Her hair is fine and glossy and one foot longer than the ordinary. She puts us to shame, her carriage is so noble. When she walks before us we feel so much in the shade that we are uncomfortable. Her mind and speech make us feel that a really noble person ought to be like her.

—If I go on describing ladies' manners I shall be

126

called an old gossip, so I must refrain from talking about those around me. I will be silent about the questionable and imperfect.

LADY KOSHŌSHŌ, all noble and charming. She is like a weeping-willow tree at budding-time. Her style is very elegant and we all envy her her manners. She is so shy and retiring that she seems to hide her heart even from herself. She is of childlike purity even to a painful degree—should there be a low-minded person who would treat her ill or slander her, her spirit would be overwhelmed and she would die. Such delicacy and helplessness make us anxious about her.

LADY MIYA-NO-NAISHI, also a beauty of good height. Her appearance as she sits is very dignified. She is fashionable. Although no single feature is especially beautiful she has altogether an air of youth and beauty. Her face is [literal translation] high in the middle and she excels others in the fairness of her skin. Her hair-ornaments, her forehead, oh, beautiful! produce an effect of refinement and elegance. She is very frank and unaffected in manner, and never the least bit awkward about anything. She is naturalness itself. Her character may be an example for us. She never tries consciously to attract, and she has no vanity.

LADY SHIKIBU is her younger sister. She is too plump, and her complexion is a fragrant white. She has a bright small face and beautiful hair, although it is not long. She presents herself before the Queen with false hair. Her plump appearance, oh, smile-giving ! Her eyes and forehead are lovely indeed ; her smile is full of sweetness.

Among the younger ladies I think KODAIBU and GEN-SHIKIBU are beautiful. The former is a little person quite modern in type. Her pretty hair is abundant at the roots, but gets too thin at the end, which is one foot longer than she is. Her face is full of wit. People will think her very pretty, and indeed there is no feature one would wish to improve. The latter is tall and rather superior. Her features are fine ; she is smile-giving and lovable. She is very refined and seems to be a favourite daughter of some person of dignity.

LADY KOHYOÉ-NO-JŌ is also refined. These ladies cannot be looked down upon by court nobles. With every one some fault is to be found, but only those who are ever mindful to conceal it *even when alone*, can completely succeed.

LADY ATTENDANT MYAKI is a very pretty person. Her hair is scarcely longer than her uchigi, the ends are beautifully cut. Her face was agreeable also when I last saw it.

There is also LADY GOSETCHI-NO-BEN.[1] She is the

[1] One of the young women who had danced the Gosetchi.

128

adopted daughter of Middle Adviser Hei. Her face is
like a picture. She has a broad forehead and eyelids
drooping at the corners. Her features are not remarkable at any point, but her complexion is white,
her hands and arms are pretty. When I saw her in
the spring for the first time her hair, which was pro-
fusely abundant, was one foot longer than herself,
but it suddenly became thinner at the ends, and now
it is only a little longer than she is.

A LADY KOMA had very long hair, an agreeable
lady in those days ; now she has become like the
bridge of a lute which has been immovably fastened
with glue. She has gone home.

So much for their appearance and now for their
dispositions. Here few can be selected, though each
has some good points and few are entirely bad. It is
very difficult to possess such qualities as prudence,
wit, charm, right-mindedness, all at once. As to
many ladies, the question is whether they excel most
in charms of mind or person. It is hard to decide!
Wicked, indeed, to write so much of others !

There is LADY CHŪJŌ who waits upon the Princess
dedicated to the service of the Kamo shrine. I had
heard of her and secretly managed to see her letters
addressed to other persons. They were very beautifully written but with such an exalted opinion of herself ; in the whole world she is the person of pro-
foundest knowledge ! None to compare with her,

it seems she is thinking. On reading them my heart beat faster, I was furiously indignant for every one here [the ladies of her own Queen's Court], although it may be it is wrong to feel so. " Be it in composition or poetry who can judge save our Princess-Abbess, who will have bright futures but the ladies attending our Princess ? " !   It may be reasonable, yet I have never seen, compared to ours, any good poems by the lady attendants of that Princess-Abbess. They seem to be living an idle poetic life, but if they were to compete with us, it is not necessarily certain they would be superior, though no one knows them well. On a beautiful moonlight night or morning, at the time of flowers or of cuckoo, courtiers might visit their residence. Other-worldly and sacred it is, and made to the taste of their Princess. There they remain undisturbed, admiring her. On the other hand, with us many things occur. The Queen has to go up to His Majesty's apartment, the Lord Prime Minister comes, and we have to keep watch at night. But there is nothing of all this in that world all their own where they may indulge in elegance and avoid blunders. If I could live there like an old piece of buried wood thrown in among them, I might succeed in freeing myself from the reproach of shallowness—would that I might indulge in elegance there, relaxing myself ! Forward young ladies there can devote themselves to dress, making themselves inferior to none and pleasing to courtiers. On the other hand, in our Queen's Court we rather neglect to adorn ourselves, for our Queen has no rivals now.

Moreover, she thinks unfavourably of frivolous women, so those who wish to serve her and remain in favour keep from association with men. Of course everywhere there are light-hearted, unashamed, thoughtless women, and men who visit our court to find them say we are awkward and unversed in social usage. Our ladies of the higher ranks are, indeed, much too reserved and haughty ; it is not in this way that they can bring honour to our Queen. It is painful to see them. The attendants of the Princess-Abbess seem to have been alluding to these ladies, but both defects and merits are found in every one, so we may not be inferior to them after all. Even our young ladies nowadays have heard of self-respect. It would be embarrassing if they were too frivolous, but one would not wish them to be heartless either.

Our Queen of perfect mind, enviably lovely, is reserved and never obtrusive, for she believes that few who are forward can avoid blunders. In fact, imperfect wit is worse than reserve. Our Queen when she was very young was much annoyed to hear persons of shallow culture saying vulgar, narrow things with conceit, so she favoured ladies who made no mistakes, and childlike persons pleased her very well. This is why our ladies have become so retiring. As Her Majesty grows older, she begins to see the world as it is, the bad and good qualities of the human heart. Reserve or boldness—she knows neither is good. The court nobles rather look down on us—" Nothing interesting here !" they seem to say. The Queen knows this, but she knows we cannot please everybody. If we stumble, hideous things may happen. Yet we must not be faint-hearted and bashful either, so Her Majesty says, but our old habits are not so easily shaken off, and all the young nobles of the present day are, on their side, only indulgent pleasure-seekers.

The ladies around the Abbess, who indulge in æsthetic pursuits, gazing at the moon and admiring flowers, may talk only of these things to the nobles, boastfully and intentionally, and the nobles might say that it is difficult to find ladies with whom they can chatter light-heartedly morning or evening, or discuss interesting topics occasionally ; although, as I have n't heard them say it, I dont' know really what they think. In general conversation it is awkward to say profound things. It is far better to speak with simplicity, and the nobles seem to think so. The difficulty is to understand the occasion and adapt one's self to it.

When the First Official of Her Majesty comes to report to her, the delicate, shy ladies-in-waiting cannot meet him on common ground, or converse fluently, not because they are deficient in words or thoughts, but because of their extreme timidity. They fear their faults may be noticed so they cannot decide what to say. Others [Abbess ladies] may not be so. Even women of high birth must follow the general custom when they become ladies-in-waiting

Of Old Japan

at the Court, but many behave as if they were still daughters at home.

The Great Adviser[1] is displeased to be received by ladies of low rank, so when he comes to the Queen's court to make some report and suitable ladies to receive him are not available, he goes away without seeing Her Majesty. Other court nobles, who often come to make reports, have each a favourite lady, and when that one is away they are displeased, and go away saying to other people, that the Queen's ladies are quite unsatisfactory. There may be some reason in it, yet it is quite unreasonable for the Abbess's ladies to say that we are unworthy to be seen or heard. It is easy to criticize, and difficult to realize our own ideals. These ladies, however, do not know that, and being full of conceit, they treat others with disdain, thus revealing their own limitations. Oh, how I wanted to show the letters to the Queen, but they had been stolen by the lady who secretly showed them to me, and they were soon taken back. I coveted those letters!

LADY IZUMI SHIKIBU[2] corresponds charmingly, but her behaviour is improper indeed. She writes with grace and ease and with a flashing wit. There is fragrance even in her smallest words. Her poems are attractive, but they are only improvisations which

[1] Fujiwara Michitaka, the Prime Minister's brother.
[2] This lady was one of the greatest poets Japan has ever produced. See her diary, which is the record of her liaison with a young prince.

drop from her mouth spontaneously. Every one of them has some interesting point, and she is acquainted with ancient literature also, but she is not like a true artist who is filled with the genuine spirit of poetry. Yet I think even she cannot presume to pass judgment on the poems of others.

The wife of the Governor of Tamba Province is called by the Queen and Prime Minister MASA HIRA EMON.[1] Though she is not of noble birth, her poems are very satisfying. She does not compose and scatter them about on every occasion, but so far as we know them, even her miscellaneous poems shame us. Those who compose poems whose loins are all but broken, yet who are infinitely self-exalted and vain, deserve our contempt and pity.

LADY SEISHONAGON.[2] A very proud person. She values herself highly, and scatters her Chinese writings all about. Yet should we study her closely, we should find that she is still imperfect. She tries to be exceptional, but naturally persons of that sort give offence. She is piling up trouble for her future. One who is too richly gifted, who indulges too much

[1] A daughter of the famous court lady, poet, and historian Akazomé Emon, to whom the court history of the time is traditionally ascribed.
[2] Seishonagon. A lady famous for her learning and wit and with a little reputation for daring. Pretty and vivacious, learned and witty, she was allowed liberties unrebuked—one may call her the New Woman of the day. She served in the court of the first Queen Sadako, daughter of the Prime Minister's brother. The two Queens were in rivalry. Seishonagon was the literary light of that court, as Murasaki Shikibu and Izumi Shikibu were of this.

in emotion, even when she ought to be reserved, and cannot turn aside from anything she is interested in, in spite of herself will lose self-control. How can such a vain and reckless person end her days happily!

[Here there is a sudden change from the Court to her own home.]

Having no excellence within myself, I have passed my days without making any special impression on any one. Especially the fact that I have no man who will look out for my future makes me comfortless. I do not wish to bury myself in dreariness. Is it because of my worldly mind that I feel lonely? On moonlight nights in autumn, when I am hopelessly sad, I often go out on the balcony and gaze dreamily at the moon. It makes me think of days gone by. People say that it is dangerous to look at the moon[1] in solitude, but something impels me, and sitting a little withdrawn I muse there. In the wind-cooled evening I play on the koto,[2] though others may not care to hear it. I fear that my playing betrays the sorrow which becomes more intense, and I become disgusted with myself—so foolish and miserable am I.

My room is ugly, blackened by smoke. I play on

[1] Because one may be bewitched; ancient belief dating from long before her day.

[2] A koto is called a horizontal harp, but it consists of a number of strings stretched the length of the instrument, the scale made by an arrangement of bridges placed under the strings, and played upon by four ivory keys worn on the four fingers of the right hand.

a thirteen or six-stringed koto, but I neglect to take
away the bridges even in rainy weather, and I lean
it up against the wall between the cabinet and the
door jamb. On either side of the koto stands a lute
[Japanese biwa]. A pair of big bookcases have in
them all the books they can hold. In one of them
are placed old poems and romances. They are the
homes of worms which come frightening us when
we turn the pages, so none ever wish to read them.
[Perhaps her own writings, she speaks so slightingly
of them.] As to the other cabinet, since the person[1]
who placed his own books [there] no hand has touched
it. When I am bored to death I take out one or two
of them ; then my maids gather around me and say :
" Your life will not be favoured with old age if you
do such a thing ! Why do you read Chinese ? Formerly even the reading of sutras was not encouraged
for women." They rebuke me in the shade [i.e.
behind my back]. I have heard of it and have wished
to say, " It is far from certain that he who does no
forbidden thing enjoys a long life," but it would be
a lack of reserve to say it [to the maids]. Our deeds
vary with our age and with the individual. Some
are proud [to read books], others look over old
cast-away writings because they are bored with
having nothing to do. It would not be becoming for
such a one to chatter away about religious thoughts,
noisily shaking a rosary. I feel this, and before my
women keep myself from doing what otherwise I

[1] Her husband who was a scholar in Chinese literature. He died in 1001.
It is now 1008.

136

MURASAKI SHIKIBU PLAYING ON A THIRTEEN-STRINGED KOTO

could do easily. But after all, when I was among the ladies of the Court I did not say what I wanted to say either, for it is useless to talk with those who do not understand one and troublesome to talk with those who criticize from a feeling of superiority. Especially one-sided persons are troublesome. Few are accomplished in many arts and most cling narrowly to their own opinion.

Pretty and coy, shrinking from sight, unsociable, proud, fond of romance, vain and poetic, looking down upon others with a jealous eye—such is the opinion of those who do not know me, but after seeing me they say, " You are wonderfully gentle to meet with ; I cannot identify you with that imagined one."

I see that I have been slighted, hated, and looked down upon as an old gossip, and I must bear it, for it is my destiny to be solitary. The Queen said once, " You were ever mindful not to show your soul, but I have become more intimate with you than others." I hope that I may not be looked at obliquely even by those who are ill-natured, affected, and unsociable. As a rule one is easy at the back [i.e. not afraid of gossip] who is modest, gentle, and of tranquil disposition. Even a coquettish and frivolous person is not rebuked if she is good-natured and of a disposition not embarrassing to others. A person who is self-exalted and eccentric with scornful mouth and demeanor can be unmistakably perceived, and one can be on one's guard ; by observing closely one

137

may discover faults of speech and behaviour. Those whose words and deeds are not in harmony, or who are always trying to outdo one another, attract notice. One seldom wishes to criticize those who have defects, but are good-natured. One cannot but sympathize with them. Those who habitually do evil with intention deserve to be freely talked about and laughed at even though sometimes they do it without intention. We ought to love even those who hate us, but it is very difficult to do it. Even the Buddha of Profound Mercy does not say that the sins against Buddha, the laws of religion, and priests, are slight. Moreover, in this muddy world it is best to let alone the persons who hate us. If we compare one who tries to excel in hatred saying extraordinary words and watching [their effect] ill-humouredly face to face, with one who coldly hides her heart with a tranquil manner, we can see which is superior.

There is a lady, Saémon-no-Naishi, who unreasonably cherished hatred of me. I was not at first aware of it, but later heard of much criticism of me in my absence. Once the King was listening to a reading of my Genji-monogatari, and said, " She is gifted, she must have read the Chronicle of Japan." This lady heard of it, and unreflectingly spread abroad among the courtiers the idea that I am very proud of my learning, giving me the name of " The Japanese Chronicle lady "—it is laughable, indeed! I am reserved even before the maids of my own house ; how then should I show my learning in Court ? When my

elder brother Shikibu-no-Jō was a boy he was taught
to read " Chinese Historical Records."[1] I listened,
sitting beside him, and learned wonderfully fast,
though he was sometimes slow and forgot. Father,
who was devoted to study, regretted that I had not
been a son, but I heard people saying that it is not
beautiful even for a man to be proud of his learning,
and after that I did not write so much as the figure
one in Chinese. I grew clumsy with my [writing]
brush. For a long time I did not care for the books I
had already read. Thus I was ashamed to think how
others would hate me on hearing what Lady Saémon
said, and I assumed an air of not being able to read
the characters written on the Royal screen. But the
Queen made me read [to her] the poetical works
of Li T'aipo, and as she wished to learn them I have
been teaching her since the Summer of two years ago
the second and third volumes of that collection very
secretly when none were present. Her Majesty and I
tried to conceal it, but His Majesty the King and the
Lord Prime Minister finding it out, the latter presented
to the Queen many poetical books which he had had
copied. I think that bitter Saémon does not know
it yet. If she did, how she would criticize me !

Everything in this world is burdensome. Now
I shall not be afraid whatever happens. Whatever
others may say of me I will recite sutras kneeling
before Amitabha Buddha.[2] When my mind has be-

[1] Large and learned volumes by the Chinese scholar Se-Mach'ien.
[2] The Merciful Buddha of the West Paradise.

come completely free from the burden of the world, nothing will weaken my determination to become a saint. Though I set myself devotedly against worldly passions, it seems that there extends before me a limbo of dull wanderings before I can mount the cloud.[1] I must be there now. I am now of a fit age for the religious life. It is common to suppose that men read sutras when they are old, yet really they are not read, for minds grow more and more relax with age. I may be interpreted as one who imitates persons of profound thought, but I will devote myself to the religious life. The person of deep-rooted sin cannot succeed even in such a hope [as that]. There happens many a circumstance which makes me think of the [probable] wickedness of my pre-natal life and everything makes me sad.

[There seems to be an abrupt transition here and the following paragraph seems to be part of a letter, perhaps sent with the diary or other writing.]

I wish I could make known everything to you, good and bad, things of the world, and those relating to my life—all that I could not write in my letters. You could not expect such writing as this from your friend ? You feel weary of life ; please look into my heart, also weary. Please write to me—even a little —whatever comes into your mind. It would be very unfortunate if my writings were scattered about and

[1] It is believed that this Buddha comes to welcome the departing soul of the believer mounted on a rainbow-coloured cloud.

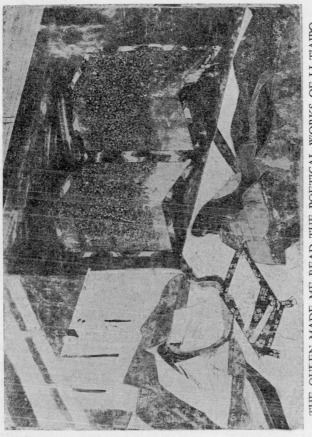

THE QUEEN MADE ME READ THE POETICAL WORKS OF LI T'AIPO.

made known to others. I have written many things of this sort, but recently I have torn up all my old writings, burying some, and making dolls' houses of the rest. Since that time I have received no letters and am determined to write no more on fresh paper, so thrifty have I become! I think I am not in the wrong. After reading, please return quickly. As I could not revise all there may be some defects ; read —overlooking them.

My mind has been wholly occupied with the things and persons of our world, and as I close this writing I reflect on how deeply rooted was my interest in them, but it was only accident that closed my descriptions of others.

[Here an interval during which she returns to Court.]

On the eleventh of the First month, 1009, in the early morning they went to the temple. The Lord Prime Minister's wife accompanied the Queen, others went by boat. I was belated and went at night. There was preaching. People made confession according to the custom of the mountain temple.[1] Many pictures of pagodas were painted, and they amused themselves. Most of the nobles had retired, and there were few persons left when the midnight preaching began. The preachers and interpreters of the sutras were twenty in number. . . . [Here is a sentence whose meaning is lost.] They all preached

[1] The great Enryakuji on Mount Hiyé, northeast of Kioto.

141

in different ways about the merit of the Queen's presence; there were many things laughed at. After the preaching the courtiers went boating; they all rowed and enjoyed themselves. At the eastern corner of the temple a bridge had been built opposite the door opening towards the North. There the High Official of the Crown Prince was leaning against the railing. The Lord Prime Minister came for a little while and talked with Lady Saishō, but as we were in the Queen's presence we could not be at our ease. It was pretty both within and without the temple. The pale moon appeared, and young nobles sang songs of the new fashion. A song related that those who had gone into the boat were young and pretty. The old Secretary of the Treasury was among them. He was ashamed with reason to sing with the others, and stood there rather embarrassed. The back view of him was comical and those within the misu [i.e. the ladies] secretly laughed. Some one said, " He in the boat is regretting old age." The High Official on the bridge heard it and sang, " The ancient seekers for eternal life—the tradition is full of lies."[1] It sounded very latest fashion, indeed. Some sang " The Duckweed " accompanied by the flute. Even the morning wind gave us unusual impressions because of the place.

In the Queen's presence was placed Genji-mono-

---

[1] A line from an old Chinese poem about Jofuku and Bunsei, seekers of the herb of eternal life. When they entered the boat they were young men, but were very old when they returned.

gatari. Once the Lord Prime Minister saw it and after many playful words wrote to me on a [poem] paper attached to a plum branch.

[The following poem depends for its point on the play upon a word with two meanings.]

Being notorious for $\begin{cases} love \\ sourness \end{cases}$
I think none pass by without breaking a branch!

[Her answer]

No one in passing has ever broken the plum tree
Who then can know if it be sour?

Oh, regrettable! to be spoken of in such a way! One night I slept in a room near the corridor. Some one came knocking at the door. I was afraid and passed the night without making a sound. The next morning the following poem was sent me [from the Prime Minister]:

All the night through, knocking louder than a water-rail,
I stood in vain at the door of hinoki wood
weary and lamenting.

I wrote back:

A cause of deep regret, indeed,
Had the door opened at the knocking of the water-rail!

[Here a space of nearly one year elapses.]

Third day of First month [1010]. The August Princes have presented themselves before the King for three days[1] to receive gifts of mochi. Ladies of high rank accompanied them. Saémon-no-Kami held the Prince, and the mochi was brought to His Majesty by the Lord Prime Minister. The King, facing towards the east door, gave it to the August Princes.[2] It was a beautiful sight to see the young Princes coming and returning through the corridor. The Queen Dowager did not present herself. On the first day Lady Saishō served at table ; her colour combination was cunningly executed. Ladies Takumi and Hyogo officiated as the Queen's secretaries. The ladies who tied their hair were particularly attractive. The lady who was entrusted with the preparation of toso[3] was very vain of her skill and behaved as if she were a doctor of medicine. Ointment was distributed as usual.

The Prime Minister took the younger Prince in his arms and the King embraced him lovingly, saying, " Long life and health " as usual. The Lord Prime Minister replied, " I will uphold the younger Prince in my arms " ; but at that His Augustness the Crown Prince became jealous and begged [to be taken up too], saying. " Ah ! Ah !" The Prime Minister was much pleased, and the General of the Right Bodyguard and others were amused by it.

The Lord Prime Minister had an audience with

---

[1] The Japanese New Year ceremonies extend over three days.

[2] Both these little princes, grandsons of the Prime Minister, eventually came to the throne.

[3] Toso :   New Year's drink of spiced saké supposed to prolong life.

the King and they came out together to find amusement. The Minister was much intoxicated. "Troublesome!" I thought, and hid myself away, but I was found. "You are summoned by the father of the Queen, yet you retire so early! Suspicious person!" said he. "Now, instead of the Queen's father it is you who must compose a poem! It is quite an ordinary occasion, so don't hesitate!" He urged, but it seemed to me very awkward to make one only to have it laughed at. As he was very much in liquor, his face was flushed and flamed out in the torchlight. He said. "The Queen had lived for years alone and solitary. I had seen it with anxiety. It is cheering to behold troublesome children on either side of her." And he went to look at the Princes, who had been put to bed, taking off the bedclothes. He was singing :

"If there be no little pines in the field
How shall I find the symbol of one thousand ages?"

People thought it more suitable that he should sing this old song than make a new one. The next evening the sky was hazy ; as the different parts of the palace are built compactly in close rows I could only catch a slight glimpse of it from the veranda. I admired his recitation of last evening with the nurse Madam Nakazukasa. This lady is of deep thought and learning.

I went home for a while. For the fifty days' ceremony of the second Prince, which was the fifteenth

day of the Sociable Month, I returned in the early
morning to the palace. Lady Koshōshō returned in
embarrassing broad daylight. We two live together; our rooms adjoin and we throw them together, each occupying the whole when the other is
absent. When we are there together we put kichō
between them. The Lord Prime Minister says we
must be gossiping about other people. Some may
be uneasy to hear that, but as there are no unfriendly
strangers here we are not anxious about it.

I went to the Queen's audience. My friend wore
brocaded uchigi of old rose and white, a red karaginu
and figured train. My dress was of red and purple
and light green. My karaginu was green and white.
The rubbed design on the train was in the very latest
fashion, and it would perhaps have been better if a
younger lady had worn it. There were seventeen
ladies of His Majesty the King's court who presented
themselves before the Queen. Lady Tachibana of
the third rank served the royal table. Ladies Kodaibu
and Shikibu on the balcony. The serving of the
young August Prince's dinner was entrusted to Lady
Koshōshō. Their Majesties sat within the dais [one
for each]. The morning sun shone in and I felt too
much brilliancy in their presence. The King wore a
robe with narrow sleeves. The Queen was dressed
in red as usual. Her inner kimonos were purple and
red with pale and dark green and two shades of yellow.
His Majesty's outer dress was grape-coloured[1] bro-

[1] The names of these colours are translated in modern terms. The

cade, and his inner garment white and green—all rare and modern both in design and colour.

It seemed to be too dazzling in their presence, so I softly slid away into an inner room. The nurse, Madam Nakazukasa, holding the young Prince in her arms, came out towards the south between the canopied King and Queen. She is short in stature, but of dignified demeanour. She was perfectly tranquil and grave and a good example for the young Prince [then not two months old!]. She wore grape-coloured uchigi and patternless karaginu of white and old rose. That day all did their utmost to adorn themselves. One had a little fault in the colour combination at the wrist opening. When she went before the Royal presence to fetch something, the nobles and high officials noticed it. Afterwards, Lady Saishō regretted it deeply. It was not so bad ; only one colour was a little too pale. Lady Kodaibu wore a crimson unlined dress and over it an uchigi of deep and pale plum colour bordered with folds. Her karaginu was white and old rose. Lady Gen Shikibu appears to have been wearing a red and purple figured silk. Some said it was unsuitable because it was not brocade. That judgement is too conventional. There may be criticism where want of taste is too apparent, but it were better to criticize manners. Dress is rather unimportant in comparison.

Japanese names of colours for dresses were all of colours in combination, which often were called after flowers or plants. These names could not convey the right idea. For instance, what is here translated *old rose and white*, would be in those days called *cherry*, intended to convey to the mind the thought of the cherry-tree in bloom.

The ceremony of giving mochi to the Prince is ended and the table is taken away. The misu of the anteroom was rolled up, and we saw ladies sitting crowded at the west side of the dais. There were Lady Tachibana of the third rank, and Naishi-no-suké, the younger attendant of the August Princes sitting in the doorway. In the east anteroom near the shioji[1] there were ladies of high rank. I went to seek Lady Dainagon and Lady Koshōshō, who were sitting east of the dais. His August Majesty sat on the dais with his dining-table before him. The ornaments of it were exquisitely beautiful. On the south balcony there sat the Minister of the Right and Left and the Chamberlain, the first officials of the Crown Prince and of the Queen and the Great Adviser Shijō, facing towards the North, the West being the more honourable seat. There were no officials of low rank. Afterwards they began to amuse themselves. Courtiers sat on the southeast corridor of the side building. The four lower officials took their usual places [on the steps below Royalty] to perform some music. They were Kagemasa, Korekazé, Yukiyoshi, Tonomasa. From the upper seat the Great Adviser Shijō conducted the music. Tō-no-Ben played the lute, Tsunetaka played the harp [koto]. The Lieutenant-General of the Left Bodyguard and State Councillor played the flute. Some outsiders joined in the music. One made a mistake in the notes and was hissed. The Minister of the Right

---

[1] Paper doors.

praised the six-stringed koto. He became too merry,
and made a great mistake, which sent a chill even to
the onlookers.

The Prime Minister's gift was flutes put into two
boxes.

III

THE DIARY OF IZUMI SHIKIBU

III

THE DIARY OF IZUMI SHIKIBU

A.D. 1002-1003

MANY months had passed in lamenting the World,[1] more shadowy than a dream. Already the tenth day of the Deutzia month was over. A deeper shade lay under the trees and the grass on the embankment was greener.[2] These changes, unnoticed by any, seemed beautiful to her, and while musing upon them a man stepped lightly along behind the hedge. She was idly curious, but when he came towards her she recognized the page of the late prince.[3] He came at a sorrowful moment, so she said, " Is your coming not long delayed ? To talk over the past was inclined." " Would it not have been presuming ?— Forgive me—In mountain temples have been worshipping. To be without ties is sad, so wishing to take service again I went to Prince Sochi-no-miya."

" Excellent ! that Prince is very elegant and is known to me. He cannot be as of yore ?" [i.e. unmarried.] So she said, and he replied, " No, but he is very gracious. He asked me whether I ever

---

[1] In the writings of the ladies of those days *World* (yononaka) is often used as a synonym of love-affair ; i.e. their relations with men.

[2] In those days noblemen's houses were surrounded with an embankment, instead of a wall.

[3] Prince Tametaka, the third Prince of the Emperor Reizei who reigned 968-969. The Prince died on June 13, 1002. He had been Izumi Shikibu's lover.

visit you nowadays—'Yes, I do,' said I; then, breaking off this branch of tachibana[1] flowers, His Highness replied, 'Give this to her, [see] how she will take it.' The Prince had in mind the old poem:

The scent of tachibana flowers in May
Recalls the perfumed sleeves of him who is no longer here.

So I have come—what shall I say to him?"

It was embarrassing to return an oral message through the page, and the Prince had not written; discontented, yet wishing to make some response, she wrote a poem and gave it to the page:

That scent, indeed, brings memories
But rather, to be reminded of that other,
Would hear the cuckoo's[2] voice.

The Prince was on the veranda of his palace, and as the page approached him with important face, he led him into an inner room saying, "What is it?" The page presented the poem.

The Prince read it and wrote this answer:

The cuckoo sings on the same branch
With voice unchanged,
That shall you know.

His Highness gave this to the page and walked away, saying, "Tell it to no one, I might be thought

[1] Tachibana: a kind of orange.
[2] The cuckoo sings when the tachibana is in flower. In this instance the "cuckoo" means the young Prince. Thus there is a suggestion here if he chooses to take it.

amorous." The page brought the poem to the lady. Lovely it was, but it seemed wiser not to write too often [so did not answer].

On the day following his first letter this poem was sent :

> To you I betrayed my heart—
> Alas! Confessing
> Brings deeper grief,
> Lamenting days.

Feeling was rootless, but being unlearned in loneliness, and attracted, she wrote an answer :

> If you lament to day
> At this moment your heart
> May feel for mine—
> For in sorrow
> Months and days have worn away.

He wrote often and she answered—sometimes— and felt her loneliness a little assuaged. Again she received a letter. After expressing feelings of great delicacy :

> [I would] solace [you] with consoling words
> If spoken in vain
> No longer could be exchanged.

To talk with you about the departed one ; how would it be [for you] to come in the evening unobtrusively ?

Her answer :

As I hear of comfort I wish to talk with you, but being an uprooted person there is no hope of my standing upright. I am footless [meaning, I cannot go to you].

Thus she wrote, and His Highness decided to come as a private person.

It was still daylight, and he secretly called his servant Ukon-no-zō, who had usually been the medium by which the letters had reached the Prince, and said, "I am going somewhere." The man understood and made preparations.

His Highness came in an humble koshi and made his page announce him. It was embarrassing. She did not know what to do ; she could not pretend to be absent after having written him an answer that very day. It seemed too heartless to make him go back at once without entering. Thinking, "I will only talk to him," she placed a cushion by the west door on the veranda, and invited the Prince there. Was it because he was so much admired by the world that he seemed to her unusually fascinating? But this only increased her caution. While they were talking the moon shone out and it became uncomfortably bright.

He : "As I have been out of society and living in the shade, I am not used to such a bright place as this"—It was too embarrassing!—"Let me come in where you are sitting ; I will not be rude as others are. You are not one to receive me often, are you?" "No, indeed! What a strange idea! Only to-night we shall talk together I think ; never again!" Thus lightly talking, the night advanced—"Shall we spend the night in this way?" he asked :

The night passes,

"HIS HIGHNESS CAME IN A HUMBLE KOSHI"

Of Old Japan

We dream no faintest dream—
What shall remain to me of this summer night?

She :

Thinking of the world
Sleeves wet with tears are my bed-fellows.
Calmly to dream sweet dreams—
There is no night for that.

He : " I am not a person who can leave my house
easily. You may think me rude, but my feeling for
you grows ardent." And he crept into the room.
Felt horribly embarrassed, but conversed together
and at daybreak he returned.

Next day's letter :

In what way are you thinking about me ? I feel anxiety—

To you it may be a commonplace to speak of love,
But my feeling this morning—
To nothing can it be compared !

She answered :

Whether commonplace or not—
Thoughts do not dwell upon it
For the first time [I] am caught in the toils.

O what a person ! What has she done ! So
tenderly the late Prince spoke to her ! She felt
regret and her mind was not tranquil. Just then the
page came. Awaited a letter, but there was none.
It disappointed her ; how much in love ! When the
page returned, a letter was given.

The letter :

Were my heart permitted even to feel the pain of waiting !
It may be to wait is lesser pain—
To-night—not even to wait for—

·The Prince read it, and felt deep pity, yet there must be reserve [in going out at night]. His affection for his Princess is unusually light, but he may be thinking it would seem odd to leave home every night. Perhaps he will reserve himself until the mourning for the late Prince is over ;[1] it is a sign that his love is not deep. An answer came after nightfall.

Had she said she was waiting for me with all her heart,
Without rest towards the house of my beloved
Should I have been impelled !

When I think how lightly you may regard me !

Her answer :

Why should I think lightly of you ?

I am a drop of dew
Hanging from a leaf
Yet I am not unrestful
For on this branch I seem to have existed
From before the birth of the world.

Please think of me as like the unstable dew which cannot even remain unless the leaf supports it.

His Highness received this letter. He wanted to come, but days passed without realizing his wish. On the moon-hidden day [last day of month] she wrote :

[1] The period of mourning was to end on June 13, 1003.

158

Of Old Japan

If to-day passes
Your muffled voice of April, O cuckoo
When can I hear?

She sent this poem, but as the Prince had many callers it could only reach him the next morning. His answer:

The cuckoo's song in spring is full of pain.
Listen and you will hear his song of summer
Full-throated from to-day.[1]

And so he came at last, avoiding public attention. The lady was preparing herself for temple-going, and in the act of religious purification. Thinking that the rare visits of the Prince betrayed his indifference, and supposing that he had come only to show that he was not without sympathy, she continued the night absorbed in religious services, talking little with him.

In the morning the Prince said : " I have passed an extraordinary night "—

New is such feeling for me
We have been near,
Yet the night passed and our souls have not met.

And he added, " I am wretched."

She could feel his distress and was sorry for him ; and said :

With endless sorrow my heart is weighted
And night after night is passed
Even without meeting of the eyelids.

---

[1] The cuckoo sings with low note in early spring, but when April is passed his voice grows clear and loud.   It is a favourite bird in Japan.

For me this is not new.

May 2. The Prince wrote to her: "Are you going to the temple to-day? When shall you be at home again?"

Answer:

In its season the time of gently falling rain will be over.
To-night I will drag from its bed the root of ayamé.[1]

Went to the temple and came back after two or three days to find a letter (from him):

My heart yearns for thee, and I wish to see thee, yet I am discouraged by the treatment of the other night. I am sad and ashamed. Do not suppose that I remain at home because my feeling is shallow.

She is cold-hearted, yet I cannot forget her.
Time wipes out bitterness, but deepens longings
Which to-day have overcome me.

Not slight is my feeling, although—

Her reply:

Are you coming?   Scarcely believable are your words,
For not even a shadow
Passes before my unfrequented dwelling.

---

[1] The meaning of the poem is vague. *Ayame* may mean *Iris sibirica*— *rain-stop, darkness*—these are homonyms in Japanese. The fifth day of the fifth month was a festival day, and people adorned their houses with *iris sibirica*, so the last line might mean that she wanted to prepare for the festival. If we take the word *ayamé* in the meaning of rain-stop, then we can understand the poem as follows: "It is the wet season now, and it is raining within my heart. To-night I am going to the temple to pray that the rainy season will be over (and to chase away the darkness from my soul). After that I wish you to come."

The Prince came as usual unannounced. The lady
did not believe that he would come at all, and being
tired out with the religious observances of several
days, fell asleep. No one noticed the gentle knocking at the gate. He, on the other hand, had heard
some rumours, and suspecting the presence of another lover, quietly retired. A letter came on the
morning of the next day :

> *I stood before your closed door*
> *Never to be opened.*
> *Seeing, it became the symbol of your pitiless heart!*

I tasted the bitterness of love, and pitied myself.

Then she knew that he had come the night before
—carelessly fallen asleep !—and wrote back :

> *How can you write the thought?*
> *The door of precious wood was closely shut,*
> *No way to read that heart.*

All is thy suspicion—O that I could lay bare my heart [to
you] !

The next night he wanted to come again, yet he
was advised against it. He feared the criticism of the
Chamberlain and Crown Prince, so his visits became
more and more infrequent. In the continuous rains
the lady gazed at the clouds and thought how the
court would be talking about them. She had had
many friends ; now there was only the Prince.
Though people invented various tales about her, she
thought the truth could never be known to any. The
Prince wrote a letter about the tedious rain :

You are thinking only of the long rains
Forever falling everywhere.
Into my heart also the rain falls—
Long melancholy days.

It was smile-giving to see that he seized upon every occasion to write her a poem, and she also felt as he did that this was a time for sentiment.

The reply :

Unaware of the sadness in your heart,
Knowing only of the rain in mine.

And on another paper she wrote another poem :

It passes, the very sorrowful life of the world—
By to-day's long $\begin{cases} \textit{rains} \\ \textit{meditation it can be known} \end{cases}$
The $\begin{cases} \textit{high-water mark} \\ \textit{flood will be exceeded.} \end{cases}$

Is it still long ? [before you come].

The Prince read this letter and the messenger came back with his answer :

Helpless man,
I am weary even of life.
Not to you alone beneath the sky
Is rain and dulness.

For us both it is a stupid world.

It was the sixth day of the Fifth month—rain not yet stopped. The Prince had been much more touched by her answer of the day before, which was deeper in feeling, and on that morning of heavy rain he sent with much kindness to inquire after her.

Very terrible was the sound of rain . . .
Of what was I thinking
All the long night through
Listening to the rain against the window?

I was sheltered, but the storm was in my heart.

The lady wrote thus to the Prince, and he thought,
" Not hopeless."
His poem :

All the night through, it was of you I thought—
How is it in a house where is no other
To make rain forgotten?

At noon people were talking about the flooding of the
Kamo River, and many went to see it, the Prince
among them.   He wrote :

How are you at present ?   I have just come back from
flood-seeing.

The feeling of my heart, like the overflowing waters of the flood,
But deeper my heart's feeling.

Do you know this ?

She wrote :

Toward me the waters do not overflow.
No depth lies there
Though the meadow is flooded.

Words are not enough.

In these words she replied to him ; and his Highness made up his mind to come, and ordered per-
fumery for himself.   Just then his old nurse, Jijū-no-
Menoto, came up : " Where are you going ? " she

said, "People are talking about it. She is no lady of high birth. If you wish her to serve you, you may summon her here as a servant. Your undignified goings-out are very painful for us. Many men go to her, and some awkward thing may happen. All these improper things are suggested by Ukon-no-Zō.[1] He accompanied the late Prince also. If you wander out in the depths of night no good can come of it. I will tell the Prime Minister[2] of the persons who accompany you in these night visits. In the world there may be changes. No one can tell what will happen to-morrow. The late Minister loved you much and asked the present one to show you favour. You must keep yourself from these indiscretions till worldly affairs are quite settled."

The Prince said: "Where shall I go? I am so bored, and am seeking temporary recreation. People are foolish to make much of it."

He said this, although much hurt by the necessity for it. Besides that, he thought her not unworthy of him and even wished to bring her to the palace [as a concubine]. On the other hand, he reflected that in that case things even more painful to hear would be said, and in his trouble of mind days were passed.

At last he visited her. "I could not come in spite of my desires. Please do not think that I neglect you. The fault is in you; I have heard that there are many friends of yours who are jealous of me. That makes

---

[1] Ukon-no-Zō, an officer in the Bodyguard. He seems to have been an attendant of the late Prince Tametaka, before he served the present Prince.

[2] Prime Minister Fujiwara-no-Michinaga, the most powerful man of the age. (See the Introduction and the Murasaki Shikibu diary.)

me more reserved, and so many days have gone by."

The Prince talked gently, and said : " Now come for this night only.   There is a hidden place no one sees ; there I can talk with tranquil mind." The koshi was brought near the veranda.   She was forced to enter it and went, without her own volition, with unsteady mind.   She kept thinking that people would know about it, but as the night was far advanced no one found them out.   The conveyance was quietly brought to a corridor where no one was and he got out.

He whispered, " As the moon is very bright, get down quickly."   She was afraid, but hurriedly obeyed him.   " Here there is no one to see us ; from this time we will meet here. At your honourable dwelling I am always anxious about other men.   I can never be at ease there."   His words were gentle, and when it was dawn he made her get into the koshi and said, " I wish to go with you, but as it is broad daylight I fear people may think I have passed the night outside the Court."

He remained in the palace, and she on her way home thought of that strange going out and of the rumours that would fly about—yet the uncommonly beautiful features of the Prince at dawn were lingering in her mind.

Her letter :

> *Rather would I urge your early return at evening*
> *Than ever again make you arise at dawn*
> *It is so sorrowful.*

His reply :

To see you departing in the morning dew—
Comparing,
It were better to come back in the evening unsatisfied.

Let us drive away such thoughts.   I cannot go out this evening on account of the evil spirit [i.e., he might encounter it].   Only to fetch you I venture.

She felt distress because this [sort of thing] could not go on always.   But he came with the same carriage and said, " Hurry, hurry ! "   She felt ashamed because of her maids, yet stole out into the koshi. At the same place as last night voices were heard, so they went to another building.   At dawn he complained of the cock's crowing, and leading her gently into the koshi, went out [with her].   On the way he said, " At such times as these, always come with me," and she—" How can it always be so ? "   Then he returned.

Two or three days went by; the moon was wonderfully bright ; she went to the veranda to see it and there received a letter :

What are you doing at this moment ?   Are you gazing at the moon ?

Are you thinking with me
Of the moon at the mountain's edge ?
In memory lamenting the short sweet night—
Hearing the cock, awake too soon !

More than usually pleasing was that letter, for her thoughts were then dwelling on the bright moon-

166

night when she was unafraid of men's eyes at the Prince's palace.

The answer:

> *That night*
> *The same moon shone down—*
> *Thinking so I gaze,*
> *But unsatisfied is my heart,*
> *And my eyes are not contented*
> *With moon-seeing.*

She mused alone until the day dawned. The next night the Prince came again, but she knew not of it. A lady was living in the opposite house. The Prince's attendant saw a koshi stopping before it and said to His Highness, "Some one has already come—there is a koshi." "Let us retire," said the Prince, and he went away. Now he could believe the rumours. He was angry with her, yet being unable to make an end of it he wrote: "Have you heard that I went to you last night? It makes me unhappy that you don't know even that.

> *Against the hill of pines where the maiden pines for me,*
> *Waves were high—that I had seen.*
> *Yet to-day's sight, O ominous !* "[1]

She received the letter on a rainy day, O unlooked-for disaster! She suspected slanderous tongues.

> *You only are my always-waited-for island—*
> *What waves can sweep it away !*

[1] In the Japanese Matsu, *n.* =pine tree; Matsu, *v.* =to wait. This poem refers to a famous one:
If my heart grows faithless, and beat for another man,
May waves pass over the hill of pines, where I pine for my beloved !

So she answered, but the Prince being somewhat troubled by the sight of the previous night, did not write to her for a long time.

Yet at last :

Love and misery in various shapes
Pass through my mind and never rest.

She wished to answer, but was ashamed to explain herself, so only wrote :

Let it be as you will, come or not, yet to part without bitter feeling would lighten my sorrow.

From that time he seldom sent letters. One moon-bright night she was lying with grieving thoughts. She envied the moon in its serene course and could not refrain from writing to the Prince :

In her deserted house
She gazes at the moon—
He is not coming
And she cannot reveal her heart—
There is none who will listen.

She sent her page to give the poem to Ukon-no-Zō. Just then the Prince was talking with others before the King. When he retired from the presence, Ukon-no-Zō offered the letter. " Prepare the koshi," he said, and he came to her. The lady was sitting near the veranda looking at the sky, and feeling that some one was coming had had the sudaré rolled down. He was not in his court robe, but in his soft, everyday wear, which was more pleasing to her eye.

He silently placed his poem before her on the end of his fan, saying, " As your messenger returned too soon without awaiting my answer—" She drew it towards her with her own.

The Prince seemed to think of coming in, but went out into the garden, singing, " My beloved is like a dew-drop on a leaf." At last he came nearer, and said : " I must go to-night. I came secretly, but on such a bright night as this none can escape being seen. To-morrow I must remain within for religious duties, and people will be suspicious if I am not at home." He seemed about to depart, when she— " Oh, that a shower might come ! So another brightness, more sweet than the heavenly one, might linger here for a while !" He felt that she was more amiable than others had admitted. " Ah, dear one," he said, and came up for a while, then went away, saying :

Unwillingly urged by the moon on her cloudy track
His body is going out, but not his heart.

When he was gone she had the sudaré rolled up and read his poem in the moonlight.

She is looking at the moon,
But her thoughts are all of me
Hearing this
It draws me to her side.

How happy ! He seemed to have been thinking her a worthless woman, but he has changed his mind, she thought. The Prince, on his side, thought the lady would have some value for him when he wanted to be amused, but even while he was thinking it, he was told that the Major-General was her favourite and visited her in the daytime. Still others said, "Hyobukyo is another of her lovers." The Prince was deterred by these words and wrote no more.

One day His Highness's little page, who was the lover of one of her maids, came to the house. While they were chattering the page was asked if he had brought a letter, he answered: "No; one day my Lord came here, but he found a koshi at the gate. From that time he does not write letters. Moreover, he has heard that others visit here." When the boy was gone this was told. She was deeply humiliated. No presumptuous thoughts nor desire for material dependence had been hers. Only while she was loved and respected had she wished for intercourse. Estrangement of any other kind would have been bearable, but her heart was torn asunder to think that he should suspect her of so shameful a thing. In the midst of mourning over her unfortunate situation, a letter was brought her:

I am ill and much troubled these days. Of late I visited your dwelling, but alas! at an unlucky time. I feel that I am unmanly.

> Let it be—
> *I will not look toward the beach—*
> *The seaman's little boat has rowed away.*

Her answer:

You have heard unmentionable things about me. I am

humiliated and it is painful for me to write any more.
Perhaps this will be the last letter.

Off the shore of { *aimlessness*
{ *Sodé*
With burning heart and dripping sleeves,
I am he who drifts in the seaman's boat.

It was already the Seventh month. On the seventh
day she received many letters from elegant persons in
deference to the celestial lovers,[1] but her heart was
not touched by them. She was only thinking that
she was utterly forgotten by the Prince, who had
never lost such an opportunity to write to her; but
[at last] there came a poem :

Alas ! that I should become like the Herder-God
Who can only gaze at the Weaving One
Beyond the River of Heaven.

The lady saw that he could not forget her and she
was pleased.

Her poem :

I cannot even look towards that shore
Where the Herder-God waits :
The lover stars also might avoid me.

His Highness would read, and he would feel that
he must not desert her. Towards the moon-hidden
day [end of the month] he wrote to her :

[1] For the Festival of the stars on the seventh day of the Seventh month
see the notes on page 24 of the Sarashina Diary. On this evening it
was customary to write letters or pay visits in memory of the heavenly
lovers.

I am very lonely.   Please write to me sometimes as to one of your friends.

Her reply :

Because you do not wake you cannot hear—
The wind is sighing in the reeds—
Ah, nights and nights of Autumn !

The messenger who took the poem came back with one from him :

O my beloved, how can you think my sleep untroubled ? Lately sad thoughts have been mine and never sleep is sound.

The wind blows over the reeds—
I will not sleep, but listen
Whether its sigh thrills my heart.

After two or three days, towards evening, he came unexpectedly and made his koshi draw into the courtyard.   As she had not yet seen him in the daylight, he was abashed, he said, but there was no help for it.   He went away soon and did not write for so long that anxiety began to fill her heart, so at last she sent :

Wearily the Autumn days drag by—
From him no message—
Boding silence !

Sweet are man's promises, but how different is the heart !

Then he wrote that, though he never forgot her, of late he could not leave the palace.

172

Of Old Japan

Though days pass
And others may forget
I can never lose the thought—
That meeting in the evening
Of an Autumn day.

The lady was pitiable, having no one to depend on, and tried to sustain herself with the uncertain consolations of a life of sentiment. Reflection increased her wretchedness, and when the eighth month came she went to Ishiyama Temple[1] to revive her doleful spirit intending to remain there for seven days.

One day the Prince said to his page : " It is a long time since I wrote ; here is a letter for her." The page replied : " I went to her house the other day and heard that she had lately gone to Ishiyama Temple." " Then—it is already late in the day—to-morrow morning you shall go there." He wrote a letter and the page went to Ishiyama with it.

Her mind was not in the presence of Buddha, but at home in the Royal City. She was thinking that were she loved by him as at the beginning there would have been no wandering like that. She was very sad, yet sadness made her pray to the Buddha with all her heart.

Perceiving that some one approached, she looked down, wondering who it might be. It was the Prince's page ! As she had just been thinking of the

---

[1] Ishiyama Temple is some five miles to the east of Kyoto. To reach there one must rise over the ascent of Osaka, and the barrier of Seki at the foot of Mount Seki, where travellers were stopped and examined. The temple commands a fine view of Lake Biwa, still more distant.

Prince, she hurriedly sent her maid to question him. The letter was brought and opened with more agitation than usual. It was as follows :

You seem to be steeped in Buddha's teaching. It would have given me pleasure to have been informed of it. Surely I am not loved so deeply that I am a hindrance to your devotion to Buddha. Only to think of your calm makes me jealous.

The poem :

> *Do you feel that my soul wanders after you,*
> *Passing across the Barrier ?*
> *O ceaseless longing !*

When shall you return ?

When she was in his neighbourhood he wrote but seldom—gratifying that he should send a letter so far ! The answer :

$$The \ way \ of \begin{cases} meeting \\ Omi^1 \end{cases}$$

She was thinking that he had quite forgotten—
Who can it be that is coming across the barrier ?

You ask when I shall go back—it is as yet uncertain.

$$On \ the \ Mount \begin{cases} Nagara \\ while \ being \end{cases}$$

$$My \ yearning \ is \ towards \ the \begin{cases} Biwa \ lake \\ open \ water \end{cases}$$

¹ This group of poems have as their base the play upon words of two meanings, or place-names whose meanings make the necessary suggestive idea. Omi is the name of the province in which are Ishiyama and Lake Biwa. Here the word is used as the homophon of meeting. Mount Nagara is near the Ishiyama Temple. *Nagara* is the homophon of " while being (on the mountain)."

174

Of Old Japan

{Uchi de no Hama
{The beach of going out

    Does not lie towards {*Miyako*
                       {*the royal city.*

The Prince read her poems and said to the page : " I am sorry to trouble you, but please go once more."

His poem :

I sought for you in the {*Osaka Yama*
                      {*mount of meeting*
But though never forgetting you
My way was lost in the trackless valley.

His second poem :

Being overwhelmed with sorrow
I wished to remain in retirement
But {*Omi no umi*
     {*the lake of meeting*
Is beyond {*Uchi de no Hama*
          {*the beach of going out.*

She wrote back only poems :

Tears which could not be restrained at the barrier
Flow towards the {*Omi no umi—*
              {*lake of meeting.*

And on the margin she wrote :

Let me try you—
My own heart also,
Come and tempt me towards the royal city.

His Highness had never thought of going so far [to seek her], but he thought he must go to her as he had received such a letter.   He came and they went back together.

His poem :

Infelicitous love!   Although entered into the Way of Eternal Law,[1]
Who was it came
And tempted back to the Royal City ?

The answer :

Out of the mountain to the darker path I wander,
Because I met you once more.

Towards the moon-hidden day a devastating wind blew hard.   It rained and she was even sadder than usual, when a letter was brought.   She thought the Prince had not lost a fit occasion to inquire for her, and she could harbour no hard thoughts of him.

His poem :

In sorrow I gaze upon the sky of Autumn
The clouds are in turmoil
And the wind is high.

Her answer :

A gentle wind of Autumn makes me sad
O day of storm—
No way to speak of it !

The Prince thought in this he could read her true feeling, but days passed before his visit.

It was after the tenth day of the Ninth month.   He waked and saw the morning moon.[2]   It seemed a

[1] Law of Buddha.

[2] The waning moon is called the morning moon because it can be seen after dawn.

176

long time since he had seen her. He felt that she was
gazing at this moon, so followed by his page, he
knocked at her gate. The lady was lying awake and
meditating, lost in a melancholy which may have
been due to the season. She wondered at the knock,
but knew not who the visitor might be. She waked
the maid lying beside her, who was in a sound sleep ;
the latter called out for the manservant. When he
went out, waking with difficulty, the knocking had
ceased and the visitor had gone. The guest must
have thought her a dull sleeper and been dishearten-
ed. Who was it likely to be ? Surely one of like
mind with herself ! Her man, who had gone out
after much rousing, and seen no one, complained that
it was only her fancy. " Even at night our mistress
is restless—Oh, these unpeaceful persons !" Thus
he grumbled away, but went to sleep again at once.

The lady got up and saw the misty sky. When
morning came she jotted down her thoughts aimlessly, and while doing it received a letter :

In the Autumn night
The pale morning moon was setting
When I turned away from the shut door.

He must have thought her a disappointing woman.
Yet she was happy to think that he never failed to
associate her with every changing season and came to
her door when he was attracted by the lovely sight of
the sky, so she folded the notes she had just written
and sent them to His Highness.

The notes :

Sound of wind; wind blows hard as if it were determined to blow away the last leaves on the branch. It grows cloudy and threatening, rain patters slightly. I am hopelessly desolate.

> *Before the Autumn ends*
> *My sleeves will be all rotted with tears,*
> *The slow rains cannot do more to them.*

I am sad, but no one remarks it; the leaves of trees and plants change day by day and so affection in him. In anticipation I feel the dreariness of the long winter rains; the leaves are pitifully teased by the winds; the drops on the leaves which may vanish at any moment—how like they are to my own life!

The sight of the leaves ever reminds me strangely of my own sadness. I cannot go within, but lie on the veranda; may-hap my end is not far off. I feel a vague anger that others are in comfortable sleep and cannot sympathize with me. Just now I heard the faint cries of wild geese.[1] Others will not be touched by it, but I cannot endure the sound.

> *How many nights, alas!*
> *Sleepless—*
> *Only the calls of the wild geese—*

Let me not pass the time in this way. I will open the shutter and watch the moon declining towards the western horizon. It seems distant and serenely transparent. There is mist over the earth; together comes the sound of the morning bell and the crowing of cocks. There will be no moment like this in past or future. I feel that the colour of my sleeves is new to me.

---

[1] Wild geese visit Japan in Autumn and fly away northwards in the early spring. They are never alone, and their cries calling to each other make the solitary woman feel loneliness more keenly.

178

"THE LADY GOT UP AND SAW THE MISTY SKY"

Of Old Japan

Another with like thoughts
May be gazing at the pale morning moon
Of the Long-night month—
No sight is more sorrowful.

Now there comes a knocking at the gate. What does it mean? Who passes the night with thoughts like mine?

There is one of like mind with me
Musing upon the morning moon.
But no way to find him out!

She had meant to send the last poem only to the Prince, but when she learned that it was His Highness himself who had come she sent all.

The Prince read and did not feel that his visit had been in vain, if she also had been awake and sadly dreaming. He wrote promptly and the letter was presented while she was gazing aimlessly. She opened it anxiously and read:

First poem:

She thinks her own sleeves only are wet
But another's also are rotting.

Second poem:

Dew-life soon to vanish away,
Hangs long suspended in forgetfulness of self
On the long-blooming chrysanthemum flower.

Third poem:

Sleepless the call of wild geese on the cloud-track
Yet the pain is from your own heart.

179

Fourth poem :

> *There may be another with thoughts like mine,*
> *Who is gazing toward the sky of the morning moon.*

Fifth poem :

> *Although not together*
> *You too were gazing at the moon*
> *Believing that I went this morning to your gate,*
>   *Alas !*

O that gate hard to be opened !

So her writing had not been uselessly sent !

Towards the moon-hidden day she had another letter.   After excusing himself for his late neglect he wrote :

I have an awkward thing to ask you.   There is a lady with whom I have been secretly intimate.   She is going away to a distant province and I want to send her a poem which will touch her heart deeply.   Everything you write touches me, so please compose a poem for me.

She was unwilling conceitedly to carry out his wishes, but she thought it too prudish to refuse him, so she wrote with the words : " How can I satisfy you ?"

Her poem :

> *In the tears of regret*
> *Your image will linger long*
> *Even after chilly Autumn has gone by.*

It is painful for me to write a heartfelt letter in your place.

And on the margin she wrote :

Leaving you, where can she go ?
For me no other life.

The Prince wrote back :

Very good poem is all that I can say. I cannot say that you have expressed my heart. Forsaking me she wanders away.

So let it be.
Let me think of you, the unexcelled one.
There is not another.

Thus I can live on.

It was the Tenth month and more than ten days had passed before the Prince came to her.

" The inner room is too dark and makes me restless. Let me sit here near the veranda." He said many heart-touching and tender words. She could not help being pleased. The moon was hidden and rain came pattering down ; the scene was in harmony with their feeling. Her heart was disturbed with mingled emotions. The Prince perceived her feeling and thought : " Why is she so much slandered by others ? She is always here alone sorrowing thus." He pitied her and startled the lady a little whose head was bowed in distress on her hand by reciting a poem :

It is not dripping rain nor morning dew
Yet here lying, strangely wet are the sleeves of the arm-pillow.

She was overwhelmed by feeling and could not

speak, but he saw her tears glistening in the moon-light. He was touched and said : " Why do you not speak ? Have my idle words displeased you ?" She replied : " I do not know why, but I feel that my heart is anguished, though your words are in my ears. You will see," she went on lightly ; " I shall never forget your poem on the sleeves of the arm-pillow."

Thus the pitiful sad night was passed, and the Prince saw that she had no other lover. He was sorry to go away from her in the early dawn, and immediately sent a message : " How are you to-day ? Are the tears dry this morning ?

Her answer :

In the morning they were dry,
For only in a dream
Were the sleeves of the arm-pillow wet.

He read it and smiled at the word " arm-pillow " which she had said she should never forget.

His poem :

You say it was only in a dream
That the sleeves were wet with tears :
Yet I cannot dry them—the sleeves of the arm-pillow.

I have never experienced so sorrow-sweet an autumnal night. Was it the influence of the time ?

After that he could not live without seeing her, and visited her oftener. As he saw her more intimately he saw that she was not a faithless woman. Her helpless situation touched his heart more and more,

"STRANGELY WET ARE THE SLEEVES OF
THE ARM PILLOW"

and he became deeply sympathetic with her. Once he said to her : " Even though you live on thus in solitude, I shall never forget you, but it would be better to come to my palace. All these slanderous rumours are due to your living alone. I for my part never met any men [here] ; is it because I come from time to time ? Yet others tell me very improper things about you which should not be heard ; it made me unspeakably sad to turn away from your shut gate. Remembering that you are living in loneliness I sometimes have made a decision ; yet being old-fashioned in my ways I hesitated to tell you of it because I anticipated the profound sadness with which you would hear these rumours ; nevertheless, I cannot continue our relations in this way. I fear that the rumour might become true ; then I should not be allowed to come, and you would become for me like the moon in the Heavenly way. If you really feel the loneliness you speak of, please come to me. There are many persons living there [in his palace], yet you will have no feeling of constraint. As I have been unhappy in my domestic relations, I do not linger in that desolate region [the house of his Princess] ; but am always alone, performing religious services ; I hope that my loneliness may be lessened by talking with you whose mind is in sympathy with mine."

Her feeling was opposed to such a thing ; she had never told him about the late Prince. Yet there was no mountain retreat to which she could fly from world-troubles and her present condition seemed like a never-ending night. There had been many men who had wanted her ; hence many strange reports were flying about. She could have confidence in no one but the Prince, so she was much tempted.

She thought : " He has his wife, yet she lives in a detached house, the nurse does all for him. If I show my affection and take pride in it, I shall be much blamed ; my wish is that he should hide me from the world."

" Though to be visited by you is a rare occurrence, such a time soothes my heart ; there is nothing else. So let anything happen, I will yield to your every wish. Elsewhere they are saying ugly things about us ; if they see the fact accomplished, how much harder their words will be !"

" Those harsh words will be said about me, not you, at any rate. I will find you a completely retired house where we can talk tranquilly." He gave her much hope, and went away in the depths of night—the barred door [outer strong gate of lattice work] had been left open [for that purpose].

She thought within herself, being much troubled : " If I continue to live alone, I can keep myself respected. If I were forsaken by him in his palace, I should be laughed at."

After she retired this poem came :

I went along the path when night was opening.
Sodden were they,
The sleeves of the arm-pillow.

184

" That idle fancy of the sleeves he has not forgotten." This pleased her.

Her poem :

Your sleeves are wet with the dews on the grass of the morning path.
The sleeves of my arm-pillow are wet, but not with dew.

The next night the moon was very bright. Here and there people were gazing at it. The next morning the Prince wanted to send her a poem and was waiting for the page [to take it]. The lady, too, had noticed the whiteness of the hoar-frost [and sent this poem] :

There was frost on the sleeves of the arm-pillow,
And in the morning,
Lo ! A frost-white world !

The Prince was sorry the lady had got ahead of him. He said to himself : " The night was passed yearning after the beloved and frost—"

Just then the page presented himself and His Highness said, with some temper, handing his letter to the page : " Her messenger has already come ; I am beaten. I wish you had come earlier." The page ran to her, and said : " I had been summoned before your messenger got there. I was late and he is angry." The lady read the letter :

The moon last night was very bright,

In a frosty morning
I await
With hope unwarranted
One who cannot be expected.

His letter seemed not to have been suggested by hers, and she was pleased that His Highness had been in the same mood with herself.

Her poem :

> *I did not sleep, gazing at the moon all night*
> *But the dawning of the day*
> *Was in whiteness of hoar-frost.*

You are angry with the page. He is very sorry, and it awakes my pity.

> *The morning sun shines on the frost*
> *So, like the sun, your face.*

Two or three days passed without a word from him. Her heart was in his promise which gave her hope, but she could not sleep for anxiety. While lying awake in bed, she heard a knocking at the gate. It was just dawn. " What can it be ?" she wondered, and sent a servant to inquire. It was the Prince's letter. It was an unusual hour for it and she wondered sorrowfully whether the Prince had been conscious of her emotion. She opened her shutter and read this letter in the moonlight :

> *Do you see that the little night opens*[1]
> *And on the ridge of the mountain, serenely bright,*
> *Shines the moon of a night of Autumn ?*

The bridge across the garden pond was clearly seen in the moonlight. The door was shut, and she thought of the messenger outside the gate and hastened her answer :

[1] It is the Japanese way to say *night opens* instead of *day dawns*. The word *little* means nothing but a feeling of endearment.

Of Old Japan

The night opens and I cannot sleep,
Yet I am dreaming dreams,
And, loving them, the moon I do not see.

The Prince thought the answer not invented, and that it would be amusing to have her near him, to respond to his every fancy. After two days he came quietly in a koshi for women. It was the first time she had shown herself to him in full[1] daylight, but it woul be unfriendly to creep away and hide, so she went to welcome him, creeping a little nearer to the entrance. He excused himself for the absence of those days and said : " Make up your mind quickly as to the thing I spoke of the other day. I am always uneasy in these wanderings, yet more uneasy when I cannot see you. O troublesome are the ways of this absurd world !"

She replied : " I wish to yield to your mind, whatever it may be, yet my thoughts are troubled when I anticipate my fate and see myself neglected by you afterwards."

He said : " Try it, I can come very seldom." And he went away. On the hedge there was a beautiful mayumi[2] and the Prince, leaning against the balustrade :

Our words are like these leaves,
Ever coloured deeper and deeper—

---

[1] The Japanese lady in her dwelling where the light was softened by her window-panes of white silk, or her sudaré, dwelt always in a sort of twilight probably very becoming to beauty.

[2] Mayumi—*Evonymæus europus*. In Autumn the leaves of the tree become purple or red, and they are so pretty that people call them "mountain brocade."

And she took it up [completing the 31-syllable poem he had begun]:

Although it is only the pearl dew that deepens them.

The Prince was pleased and thought her not without taste.

He seemed very elegant. He was attired as usual, his underdress exquisite. Her eye was much charmed, and she thought that she was too frivolous [to be thinking about it].

Next day he wrote:

Yesterday I was sorry that you were embarrassed, yet the more attracted by it.

She answered:

The Goddess of Mount Katuragi[1] would have felt so too—
There is no bridge across the way of Kumé.

I did not know what to do.

The messenger came back with his poem:

Were my devotion to be rewarded
How could I stop,
Though bridge were none at Katuragi San.

---

[1] According to an ancient fable, En-no-Shōkaku, a great magician who could command even gods, once summoned gods of many mountains to make a stone bridge at Kumé on Mount Katuragi in the Province of Yamato. The goddess of Mount Katuragi was very shy, and, working only at night, never showed herself before others. The magician grew angry with her, and punished her by unveiling her. That was the cause of the failure in the work. (The inmost soul hides itself and works in the dark. If you try to bring it into clear consciousness, you will fail in your work.)

Of Old Japan

After that he came oftener, and her tiresome days were lightened.

But her old friends also sent letters and visited her, too, so she wanted to go to the Prince's palace at once, lest some unlucky thing should occur; yet her heart was anxious and hesitating.

One day he sent word: " Maple trees of the mountain are very beautiful. Come! let us go together to see them." She answered, " I shall be glad to do it." But the appointed day came and his Highness wrote: "To-day I must confine myself for a religious service." But that night it stormed, and the leaves were all gone from the trees. She waked and wrote to the Prince how sorry she was that they could not have gone the previous day.

His answer:

> In the Godless month[1] it stormed—
> To-day I dream and dream
> And wonder if the storm was within my heart.

She returned:

> Was it a rainstorm? How my sleeves are wet!
> I cannot tell—but muse profoundly.

After the night storm there are no more maple leaves. O that we could have gone to the mountain yesterday!

His Highness returned:

O that we might have gone to see the maple leaves, for this morning it is useless to think of it.

[1] The Godless month—the Tenth month; so called because in that month all the gods left their abodes and went to the High Plain of Heaven to hold counsel together.

And on the margin there was a poem :

> *Though I believe*
> *No maple leaves are hanging on the boughs,*
> *Yet we may go to see*
> *If scattering ones remain.*

And she answered :

> *Were the mountains of evergreens to change into red leaves,*
> *Then we would go to see them*
> *With tranquil, tranquil hearts.*
> My poem will make you laugh !

The night came and the Prince visited her. As her dwelling was in an unlucky direction,[1] he came to take her out of it.

"For these forty-five days I shall stop at my cousin's, the Lieutenant-General of the Third Rank, on account of the unlucky direction [of my own house]. It is rather embarrassing to take you to that unfamiliar place." Yet he dared to take her there. The koshi was drawn into its shelter [small house built for it]; the Prince got out and walked away alone, and she felt very lonesome. When all were asleep he came to take her in and talked about various things. The guards, who were curious about it, were walking to and fro. Ukon-no-Zō and the page waited near the Prince. His feeling for her was so

---

[1] In those days they believed in lucky and unlucky directions. Those who went in an unlucky direction might have some unfortunate incidents. This belief still holds in the country life of the people. The writer was once deprived of a good servant who wanted to come to her, but could not because her house was in an " unlucky direction ."

intense at this moment that all the past seemed dull. When day dawned he took her back to her own home, and hurriedly returned himself to get back before people woke up.

She could no longer disregard the earnest and condescending wish of His Highness, and she could no more treat him with indifference. She made up her mind to go to live with him. She received kind advice against it, but did not listen. As she had been unhappy, she wanted to yield herself to good fortune ; yet when she thought of the court servitude she hesitated and said to herself : " It is not my inmost wish. I yearn for a retired religious life far away from worldly troubles. What shall I do when I am forsaken by the Prince ? People will laugh at my credulity. Or shall I live on as I am ? Then I can associate with my parents and brothers ; moreover, I can look after my child,[1] who seems now like an encumbrance." Nevertheless, at last she wanted to go, and she did not write her heart to the Prince, for she thought he would know everything about her if they should live together. Her old friends sent letters, yet she did not answer them saying [to herself] : " There is nothing to write."

A letter from the Prince—in it was written : " I was a fool to believe in you." His words were few. There was an old poem :

---

[1] In 997 she had Koshikibu-no-Naishi (she was also a poetess and court lady). Her husband was Tachibana Michisada, to whom she was married before she knew Prince Tametaka.

You are faithless, yet I will not complain.
As the silent sea
Deep is the hate in my heart.

Her heart was broken. There were many extraordinary rumours about her, yet there were days when she believed that no harm could come of a false rumour. Some one must have slandered her, suspecting that she was yielding to the earnest desires of the Prince and going to live at the palace.

She was sad, but could not write to him. She was ashamed to think of what the Prince might have heard. The Prince, seeing that she did not explain herself, wrote to her again :

Why do you not answer ? Now I believe in the rumour. How swiftly your heart changes ! I heard something I did not believe, and wrote to you that you might wipe away such unpleasant thoughts from my mind.

These words opened [i.e. lightened] her bosom a little. She wanted to know what he had heard and suddenly the wish to see him came to her.

O could you come to me this instant ! I hunger to see thee, but cannot go because I am buried in slander.

The Prince wrote back :

You are too afraid of slanders and I read your mind in this caution. I am angry about it.

She thought he was teasing her, yet it saddened her, and she replied :

I cannot help it, please come in any case !

192

He returned :

I say to myself, " I will not suspect, I will not resent,' but my heart does not follow my will.

Her answer :

Your enmity will never cease. I rely upon you, yet I suspect your faithfulness.

In the evening the Prince came. He said : " I wrote to you not believing the story. If you wish not to have such things said of you, come !"

She replied : " Then take me there !" But when it was dawn His Highness returned alone. He wrote to her continually, yet he seldom visited her. Once there was a great storm—the Prince did not inquire for her. She thought His Highness did not sympathize with her solitude, so wrote to him in the evening :

> *The season of the withering frost is sad,*
> *The autumnal wind rages*
> *And the sighing of the reed never stops.*

The Prince's answer was :

> *The solitary reed which none but me remembers*
> *How it is sighing in the raging wind !*

I am even ashamed to confess how much my mind is completely occupied with you.

She was pleased, indeed. The Prince sent his koshi, saying that he was going to the hidden rendezvous to avoid the unlucky direction of his house. The lady went thither, thinking she would follow every wish of his.   They talked tranquilly for many days and nights, and her unrest was chased away.   She was now not unwilling to live with him, but when the time for avoiding the unlucky direction was over, she was sent back to her home.   There she thought of him more longingly than ever, and sent a poem :

In this hour of longing
Reflection brings to mind each day gone by
And in each one
Was less of sorrow.

He replied :

Sorrows of love were less each yesterday,
But how can those vanished days be caught again?

There is no other way but to resolve to come to me.

She was still cautious and could not take things so easily.   She passed many days in musing.   By this time the coloured leaves [of Autumn] had all fallen. The sky was clear and bright.   One evening as the sun was setting she felt very lonely and wrote to him :

You are always my consolation,
Yet with the end of day sadness comes.

He replied :

All are sad when the day ends,
Yet are you sadder than any—
You who wait?

I can sympathize with you and I am coming.

194

The next morning the frost was very white; he sent to inquire for her, asking, " How are you feeling now ?"   She sent a poem :

> *Not in repose was the night passed ;*
> *But the frosty morning*
> *Brought its own charm,*
> *Incomparable.*

His answer contained many touching words, and a poem :

> *To think alone is [not life].*
> *If you were thinking the same thoughts—*

She answered :

> *You are you and I am I,*
> *Yet between your heart and mine is no separation.*
> *Make no such distinctions.*

The lady caught cold.   Though not serious she suffered.   The Prince often inquired for her and at last she answered, saying :

A little better.   The thread of life thinned down and it seemed to be going to break, but now it is dear to me because of you.   It is because I am deep in sin ?

He wrote back :

> *Gladly do I hear it :*
> *The thread of your life*
> *Cannot easily be broken,*
> *For it is tied together,*
> *With pledges of long-enduring affection.*

The end of the year was at hand. The first day of the Frost month seemed like a day of early spring, but the next morning it snowed. The Prince sent a poem :

> *Since the god-age it has snowed,*
> *It is a known thing,*
> *Yet that snow seems very fresh this morning !*

She returned an answer :

> *First snow ! I see it young every winter,*
> *Yet my face grows old*
> *As Winter comes.*

Days were passed in exchanging these nothings. Again his letter :

I become impatient to see you, and just now wanted to go to you, but my friends have met here to compose poems together.

She wrote :

> *Had you no time to come ?*
> *Then I would go to you.*
> *O that I knew* $\begin{cases} \text{an even way of love.} \\ \text{the art of composing poems.} \end{cases}$

He was pleased.

Come to my house. Here is the even way and here's the way to see each other.

That night he visited her, and talked touchingly of many things. " Would you be sad," he said, " if I should desert my house and become a monk ?" He spoke sadly, and she wondered why such a thought

196

had entered his mind, and whether it could be true or not. Overcome with melancholy she wept. Outside was tranquil rain and snow : they slept not at all, but talked together with feeling throughout the night as if the world were all forgotten. She felt that his affection was deeper than she had suspected. He seemed to feel everything in her, and could sympathize with her every emotion. In that case she could accomplish her determination from the beginning [to go to become a nun]. So she made up her mind, but said nothing and sat lamenting. He saw her feeling and said :

Lovers' fancy of a moment held us both through the night,

And she continued :

> *Tears came to their eyes,*
> *And without was the rain.*

In the morning he talked of merrier things than usual, and went back. Though she had no faith in it [i.e. the convent], yet she had been thinking of it to comfort her solitude. Now her mind was confused, trying to think how to realize it, and she told her perplexed feeling to the Prince :

> *On waking I cannot think.*
> *I wish that those were only dreams [of which we talked last night].*

And on the margin she wrote :

> *We made our vows so earnestly,*
> *Yet must these vows yield*
> *To the common fate of the changing world.*

197

I am sorry to think of it.

The Prince read it and made answer :

I wanted to write to you first—

I will not think it real,
Those sad things were only dreams
Dreamed in a night of dreams.

I wish that you would think so too.   You dwell too much upon nothing.

Only life is fickle :
We know not how it will end.
But promises shall endure
As long as the pine-tree at Suminoyé.[1]

O my beloved, I spoke to you of what I did not heartily wish.   You are too literal.   I am sorry for that.

Yet the lady's thought lingered over that sad intention and she lamented much.   Once she was making haste to set out when she received the Prince's letter :

Oh, I longed for it, though I had just seen it
A yamato-nadeshiko[2] growing in the hedge of a mountain-
dwelling.

It was painful to her present mind, yet she replied :

If you love, come and see,
Even the thousand swift gods will not forbid
Those who follow in the Way.

[1] The pine-tree at Suminoyé is famous for its age.
[2] Yamato-nadeshiko—a Japanese pink ; the homonym means the caressed girl of Yamato.

Of Old Japan

He smiled over the poem. As he was reading sûtras those days he sent the following poem:

> *The way of meeting is not god-forbidden.*
> *But I am on the seat of the Law*
> *And cannot leave it.*

Her answer:

> *Then will I go thither to seek you,*
> *Only do you enlarge the seat!*

Once it snowed heavily and he sent her a poem affixed to a branch covered with snow:

> *Snow falls, and on all the branches*
> *Plum flowers are in bloom,*
> *Though it is not yet spring.*

This was unexpected and she wrote back:

> *Thinking that plum flowers were in bloom*
> *I broke the branch,*
> *And snow scattered like the flowers.*

The next morning early he sent a poem:

> *These winter nights lovers keep vigil.*
> *Lying on one's lonely bed*
> > *Day dawns*
> *And the eyelids have not met.*

Her answer:

> *Can it be true?*
> *On Winter nights eyes are shut in ice [frozen tears]*
> *And midnight hours are desolate.*
> *I wait for dawn, although no joy is in it.*

199

What the Prince had been thinking of he wrote in heart-dwindling words, saying, " I think I cannot live out my life in this world," so she wrote back :

> *For me, it is fitting to speak of these things,*
> *For they recall*
> *The romance of past days.*

His poem :

> *I would not exist even for a moment*
> *In a world where sorrows*
> *Follow one another like the joints*
> *In the bamboo stalk.*

He had been troubling himself to find out a fit place to conceal her, but he reflected, " She is not used to such a life and would be embarrassed by it. For my part, I should be much rebuked. It is simpler to go myself and bring her as my maid."

So on the eighteenth of the Finishing month on a moon-bright night he visited her. He said in the ordinary way, " Now, please come," and she thought it for a night only. When she got into the koshi alone, " Take an attendant with you. If you are willing we will talk together tranquilly to-morrow and the day after to-morrow."

He had not spoken in this way before, and she, guessing his intention, took her maid with her. She was not carried to the same house as before. The room was beautifully adorned, and he said, "Live here privately ; you may have several attendants." Now she was sure she had understood him and she thought it fortunate to come thus secretly. People would be

"IN THE DAYTIME COURTIERS CAME TO SEE HIM"

astonished to find she had come here to live before they were aware. When day dawned she sent her servant to fetch her case of combs and other things. The Prince left the room, but the shutters were still closed. It was not frightful, but uncomfortable.

"I wish," said the Prince, "to arrange that you shall live in the North building. This room is near the Audience Room and has no charm in it" [i.e. some one might discover her]. So she shut herself up and listened in secret. In the daytime courtiers of the ex-Emperor (his father) came to see him. He said: "How is it with you here? Can you stay? I feared that you would find it disagreeable by my side"; and she answered, "I feared just the same thing." He laughed and said: "To tell the truth, take care of yourself while I am away; some impertinent fellows may come to catch a glimpse of you. In a few days I will have you live openly in the room where now is my housekeeper [nurse]. The room where I pass the day has no visitors."

After two or three days she was removed to the North side building.[1] People were astonished and ran and told the Princess, who said: "Even without this event, I have not been treated as I ought to have been. She is of no high birth; it is too much." She was angry because he had told her nothing. His secrecy displeased her very much, and she was more inconsolable than ever. The Prince felt sorry for her and tried to be with her oftener. She said to him:

[1] See plan of palace or nobleman's house.

"I am ill with hearing rumours and have come to hate seeing people. Why have you not told me this before? I would not have interfered: I cannot bear to be treated like a woman of no importance. I am ashamed to think that people are laughing at me." She said it weeping and weeping. He answered: "I brought her for my maid, and I thought that you would allow it; as you are angry with me the Lieutenant-General [her brother] hates me also. I brought her to dress my hair and she shall serve you also." The Princess was not softened by these words, but she was silenced.

Thus days passed and the lady became used to the court life. She dressed his hair and served in everything. As he did not allow her to retire to her private room, the visits of the Princess became more and more rare. The Princess lamented it infinitely. The year turned back and on the first day of the Social month all the courtiers came to perform the ceremony of congratulation before the Emperor. The Prince was among them. He was younger and fairer than any, and even this made her ashamed of herself. From the Princess's house her ladies went out to see the procession, yet they did not care so much to see the courtiers as to look at her. They were in great disorder looking about; it was an ugly sight.

After dark when the ceremony was over, His Highness came back and all the court nobles came with him to amuse themselves. It was very gay and a contrast to the solitary life of her old home. One day the Prince heard that even the lowest servants were speaking evil of her. He thought it was due to the behaviour of his wife, and being displeased seldom went to the Royal dwelling. She was sorry for the Princess, yet she did not know what to do. She remained there, thinking that she would do as she was bid.

The Princess's elder sister was married to the Crown Prince and just then was living with her parents. She wrote to the younger Princess : " How are you ? I have heard something of what people are saying these days. Is it true ? Even I feel disgraced. Come to us during the night."

The Princess could not console herself when she thought how much people who make talk about nothing were gossiping. She wrote back to her sister : " I have received your letter. I had been unhappy in the world [married life] and now am in a painful situation. For a time I will go back, and the sight of the young Princess will comfort me. Please send some one to summon me. I cannot go away when I desire, for he will not permit it." She began to put her affairs in order, taking away those things which must not be seen by others. She said : " I am going there for a while, for if I stay here my husband will feel uncomfortable to come to me. It is painful for both of us." And they said : " People are talking and laughing about it a good deal. He went out himself to get her. She is dazzling to the eye ; she lives in the court ladies' room over there. She goes to the Prince's hall three or four times a day. It is quite right that you should punish him—going away with few words!"

All hated the lady, and he was sorry for her. His Highness suspected what his wife was going to do, and he found his conjecture realized when the sons of his brother-in-law came to fetch her. A lady-in-waiting said to the housekeeper : "The princess has taken important things with her ; she is going away." The housekeeper was in great anxiety and said to the Prince : "The Princess is going away. What will the Crown Prince think of it ! Go to comfort her."

It was painful to her [the lady] to see these things going on. She was very sorry and pained, yet, as it was an unfit time to say anything, she kept silence. She wanted to get away from this disagreeable place, but thought that also not good. She thought she could never get rid of her trouble if she stayed. His Highness went towards the Princess, who met him as if nothing had happened. "Is it true," he said, "that you are going to your elder sister ? Why have you not asked me for the koshi ?" She answered : "Something has happened. There is something which demands me and they have sent messengers for me." She said nothing more. The Princess's words, her letters, and those of her sister were written roughly, from supposition.

THE END

APPENDIX

APPENDIX

A

OLD JAPANESE CALENDAR

THE year was divided according to a Lunar Calendar, which was one month or so in advance of the present Solar Calendar.

NAMES OF THE MONTHS

First month; Social month; Spring-birth month.

Second month; Clothes-again-doubled month; Little-grass-growing month.

Third month; Ever-growing month; Flowery month; Dreaming month.

Fourth month; Deutzia month; First Summer month.

Fifth month; Rice-sprout month; Tachibana month.

Sixth month; Watery month (rice-fields filled with water).

Seventh month; Rice-ear month; Literary month (people composed poems on the star festival).

Eighth month; Rice-ear-swelling month; Mid-autumn.

Ninth month; Chrysanthemum month; Long-night month.

Tenth month; Gods-absent month; Thunderless month; Little Spring.

Eleventh month; Frost month.

Twelfth month; Last month; Spring-waiting month.

B

CHRONOLOGICAL TABLE OF EVENTS CONNECTED WITH THE DIARIES

974. Izumi Shikibu, the daughter of Ōé Masamuné, Governor of the Province of Echizen, born.

977. Prince Tametaka (future lover of Izumi Shikibu) born.

978. Prince Atsumichi (future lover of Izumi Shikibu) born.
Murasaki Shikibu, daughter of Fujiwara Tametoki, born.

980. Prince Yasuhito (afterwards the Mikado Ichijo) born.

988. Akiko, Michinaga's first daughter, born.

990. Sadako, daughter of Michinaga's eldest brother Michitaka, comes to the Court, and later becomes Queen to Mikado Ichijō.

991. Sei-Shōnagon comes to Court as one of Queen Sadako's ladies.

994. Prince Atsumichi comes of age and marries the third daughter of Michitaka.

995. Izumi Shikibu marries Tachibana Michisada.
Prince Atsumichi divorces his first wife.

996. Prince Atsumichi marries again.

997. Murasaki Shikibu goes to Echizen with her father who has been made Governor of the Province.
Akiko joins the Court.
Izumi Shikibu's first daughter born.

998. Murasaki Shikibu returns to Kyoto.

999. Murasaki Shikibu marries Fujiwara Nobutaka.

Appendix

1000. Akiko made second queen.
 Murasaki Shikibu's daughter born.
1001. Pestilence.
 Murasaki Shikibu's husband dies.
 Conflagration of the Palace.
1002. Murasaki Shikibu probably began the writing of the
 " Genji Monogatari."
 Sei-Shōnagon probably began the " Makura-no-
 Sōshi."
 In June, Prince Tametaka (Izumi Shikibu's lover ;
 (her husband, from whom she was divorced, had
 died earlier) dies.
 Izumi Shikibu begins a liaison with Prince Atsumichi.
1003. Izumi Shikibu goes to live at the South Palace.
1004. Izumi Shikibu leaves Prince Atsumichi's palace, and
 marries Fujiwara Yasumasa.
1005. Murasaki Shikibu joins the Court.
 Conflagration of the Palace.
 Izumi Shikibu goes to the Province of Tango, her
 husband having been appointed Governor.
1007. Akiko (second queen) gives birth to Prince Atsu-
 sada.
 Murasaki Shikibu begins to keep her diary.
1008. Izumi Shikibu returns to become lady-in-waiting at
 the Court.
1009. Fujiwara Takasué's daughter (author of Sarashina
 Diary) born.
1017. Fujiwara Takasué being appointed Province
 Governor, goes to his province with his daughter.
1021. Takasue's daughter returns to Kyoto. Sarashina
 Diary begun.

KENKYUSHA CO. PRESS
TOKYO, JAPAN